YOUNG BY NAME

Whimsical Columns from the

Tetbury Advertiser

DEBBIE YOUNG

YOUNG BY NAME

Whimsical Columns from the *Tetbury Advertiser*

by Debbie Young

Published by Hawkesbury Press 2016

Hawkesbury Upton, Gloucestershire, England

The content of this book has previously appeared on Debbie Young's website: www.authordebbieyoung.com.

Cover image by the author's father Peter

Exterior and interior design by the author

ISBN 978-1-911223-03-0

Also available as an ebook

To the Tetbury Lions

who publish ten jam-packed issues

of the Tetbury Advertiser *every year*

Thank you for hosting my monthly column

and for all that you do for the community

Contents

Foreword

The Advertiser has been around for over forty years now. I delivered it by bicycle when we were both in our formative years. I ignored it in my teens (it had no Punk Rock or New Wave stories) then returned to it avidly later, using it as a lifeline to the old home town during an absence in Swindon, the big city. It's been to America with me, during the "paper" years it was the go-to source to absorb paint spills, and it's always been a smallest-room accessory. I now find myself editing it – may wonders never cease.

During those long ages there have been a number of professional and semi-professional writers who've helped prop the thing up with their verdant prose. The serendipity of Roseblade, the keen comment of Gibbs, the steady input of Aunt Sally and more – all have helped keep it relevant and readable. The latest and most eloquent of all, the "Jewel in the Crown" of any current *Advertiser* offering, is of course the wonderful Debbie Young. The quality of her submissions makes my life simultaneously much easier as editor and hugely enriched as a reader. I hope you enjoy this collection as much as I have. Long may she reign!

Richard Smith, Editor, Tetbury Advertiser

Foreword

Introduction

In the same month that I started my writing blog, I penned my first monthly column for the *Tetbury Advertiser.* My column shared the name of my writing blog, "Young By Name", and for me it feels as significant a part of my writing career as that blog.

The editors have kindly given me free rein to write about any subject, and the columns reflect my butterfly mind, although often topical and Tetbury-focused. I am very grateful to the *Advertiser*'s kind and patient editors – first Barry Gibbs then Richard Smith – for their generous support and encouragement, and I am in awe of the amazing job they do on behalf of the Tetbury Lions, producing their excellent community magazine each month, which raises thousands of pounds for local charities. It is a very worthy recipient of the Queen's Award for Voluntary Service, and I feel privileged to have played a part in the magazine's success for the last six years.

Although I share my columns on my blog once they've appeared in the *Advertiser*, I wanted to bring them together in a single volume for a selfish reason: rereading them provides a record of my personal history. But also it documents many historic moments and social changes which I hope residents of Tetbury, Gloucestershire and the wider world may enjoy. Today is tomorrow's history, and I am glad to have the opportunity to be its recorder.

Debbie Young

Spring Cleaning

March 2010

As the early spring sunshine streams in through my daughter's bedroom window, I scoop up a half-dressed Barbie from the floor. Tidying her bedroom is going to be a lengthy job. To imagine the state of her room at this stage, picture what would happen if you took a giant food blender, filled it with hundreds of toys, then started the motor without putting the lid on. You get the idea.

I've tried blaming her father.

"I think Laura has inherited your tidiness gene," I tell him.

"I don't think I've got one," he says.

"Exactly my point."

My mother thinks it's my fault.

"When you were her age, I had to bribe your big sister to tidy your room."

At least I didn't have such a huge quantity of toys to put away. I could count the number of dolls I possessed on one hand, whereas Laura would need a football team to ensure sufficient fingers. I had just three shelves of books and knew every page practically by heart; many of Laura's dozens of books have barely been opened. My pencil case was a lone creature, but my daughter's apparently flock. To me, a good collection of colouring pencils meant a set of ten, whereas hers run to about 100. As to felt tip pens, I think they breed after dark. My heart leaps each time one runs out, because it means I can throw it in the bin with a clear conscience, but still they multiply.

I remember the invention of felt tips when I was small and the excitement of buying my first pack, which held just four. They were expensive, costing two shillings, and I paid with the pre-decimal pennies that my grandfather used to save for me in a jar – a special treat to help fill the void between Christmas and birthdays.

So where do all Laura's toys come from? Free activity packs at family restaurants certainly account for the stationery glut. Another new source is the charity shop. There were none my local high street when I was a child, but now they spring up all over the place. Don't get me wrong, I applaud them – they do a fabulous job, fundraising and recycling at one fell swoop. Shopping in them is a very easy way to support a worthwhile charity, so I tend to give Laura free rein. Progressing now on hands and knees through the carpet of toys in her bedroom, I realise that this is my undoing.

In my day, old toys weren't taken to the charity shop but went into the dustbin (we didn't worry about landfill in the 60s) or were collected for scrap by the rag-and-bone-man. This was the fate of my beloved push-along Baa-Lamb when I was about four, and I've never forgiven my mother.

These days, old toys never die – they just relocate to Laura's bedroom.

Happy Spring Cleaning!

Laura's Ambition

April 2010

On holiday at half term, my six-year-old daughter Laura discovered a new career and added it to her list of what she wants to be when she grows up. So far, her ambitions have all been chosen without any prompting from me: bus driver, "Rainbows lady", teacher, art gallery owner, taxi driver.

Not long ago, I watched a documentary about mothers who made career plans for their toddlers. One had decided that hers would be a doctor. Whether as an adult he would have the aptitude, skills or desire did not matter. She had made up her mind, keen to fulfil her own thwarted ambitions through her child. I'm determined not to fall into that trap. Born in 21st century Britain, Laura can choose her own career freely, even though she was born a girl.

Things were different for her great grandmothers, her grandmother and even for me. My grandmothers were constrained by their era. One longed to be a teacher, but female teachers were not allowed to marry and she considered herself lucky to have a husband instead of a career. So many of her contemporaries had lost their sweethearts in the Great War. My other grandmother wanted to be a nurse, but early marriage and an unstoppable succession of children put paid to that idea. She would have been a natural. When, at the age of eight, I trod on a rusty nail in bare feet, she managed to remove it without hurting me. I watched in awe and said to her:

"You really ought to have been a nurse."

She looked very wistful.

My mother gave greater priority to her career but did not stray from traditional women's professions. She was a secretary before I was born and trained as a teacher once I'd started nursery. In the 1960s, for a mother of three, even that was considered radical.

My own career was launched on the cusp of women's equality in the workplace. The theory was in place, but the practice was a little patchy (and still is). But it was not the workplace that held me back, but our school careers advice. In those days, careers duties fell to the teacher with the lightest teaching load. At our girls' grammar school, this meant the RE mistress, who knew very little of the world of work and held our careers interviews in a store cupboard. The only advice that I remember was "Don't go to York University – it's an awfully long way from home". She meant well, but I'm glad I had the confidence to disregard her.

Most of my classmates complied with her recommendations and became teachers or secretaries. Surprisingly none became nuns, but one girl is nearly a vicar. Even the RE teacher could not have recommended this career, because at that time it wasn't open to women. Another girl rendered the poor lady speechless by enquiring about opportunities in the oldest profession. I found out on Facebook recently that she's now a personal trainer, and I don't think that job existed even for men in those days. And in the 1970s it would have taken a psychic to predict the 21st century demand for website designers.

I wonder whether my daughter will also end up in a career that has yet to be invented. Perhaps she'll be a spaceflight attendant, a time-travel agent or an invisibility cloak seamstress – Who knows what opportunities new technology will bring? But for the moment, Laura's heart is set on the career she discovered on Barcelona beach at half-term.

"Mummy, I think I'll be a person who builds giant models out of sand and then people have to put money in their bucket."

Well, some old professions never really lose their charm.

May Day

May 2010

For me, the concept of May Day will be forever associated with an annual ritual that took place at my infant school in Sidcup, a Kentish suburb of London.

Each May Day, or the closest school day to it, the girls from the oldest class became "May Maidens". We had to dress in white frocks, and the prettiest girl (how un-PC is that?) was crowned May Queen. A determined band of mothers raided everyone's gardens for roses and greenery to make into wreaths for the Maidens' hair; they also wove two long floral ropes for the Maidens to carry.

For the May Day ceremony, the whole school turned out onto the field. "The Elizabethan Serenade" played over the tannoy, while two lines of May Maidens, each carefully carrying one of the ropes, processed slowly to the far end of the field. Then they stood still while the May Queen and two attendants proceeded down the length of the floral aisle. Once the May Queen had taken her place on her throne, the Maidens sat down on the grass and the Headmistress addressed the gathered crowd of parents and children.

I don't remember what the boys had to do, but they must have found the whole thing pretty dull. Not so the mothers, who ooh'd and aah'd as we walked by, snapping away with big, boxy cameras.

Those were gentler days, I think to myself, wishing that my own small daughter had the chance to take part in such an idyllic ritual. But then I realise with a start that the backdrop to this quaint ceremony was far from idyllic. For behind where the May Maidens sat, all along the edge of the school field, was a long row of air-raid shelters. Though the war was over long before we May Maidens were born, most of the adults watching our procession would have been all too familiar with the inside of an air-raid shelter.

Funny how it seems it was always summer when I was a child...

These days it is hard to imagine that Health and Safety inspectors would allow any school to have such dark, dingy unlit sheds on the school field. Risk assessment for air raid shelters? There's an interesting thought. In those days, of course, children were allowed to enjoy a little danger, but I'm sure that's not the only reason the shelters were retained. I suspect there was an inkling that we might needed to use them again. This was, after all, the 1960s. The Cold War was in full swing. Even as recently as 1980, the government was issuing its infamous "Protect and Survive" leaflets, telling us how to guard against a nuclear attack. (Unbelievably, top tips were to sit under the kitchen table, or to take a door off its hinges if a table wasn't to hand.)

We live in more peaceful times. My daughter may not get to be a May Maiden, but at least I don't have to worry about a bomb falling on her school. All the same, she'd look awfully pretty with roses in her hair.

Young Voters

June 2010

In the run up to last month's general election, I felt it was my maternal duty to make my small daughter aware that she was living through a historic moment.

I have a few memories of national and international import from my own childhood. Kennedy's assassination, chiefly because it was the only time our next door neighbour came in to our house unannounced and the only time I saw her cry. Winston Churchill's funeral: I had no idea who he was, but I knew that he was A Great Man. The first footstep of mankind on the moon: unlike most British children, I experienced this in the afternoon, because at that point my family lived in California.

So I had not expected Laura to be especially interested in the election, especially considering her school, unlike her cousin's, was not closed for the day to be used as a polling station. (What a great way to instil a love of democracy in young children.) To my surprise, she followed the election news avidly and quickly formed strong and independent political views.

Firstly, she favoured Gordon Brown as "president" because he shared a Christian name with her Daddy. Then she clamoured for an orange diamond on a stick to be displayed in our front garden because her best friend had one in hers. She liked the local Lib Dem's alliterative slogan: "Win With Webb" and was gratified when he did.

"Why don't they make Win With Webb president?" she asked. "He sounds good."

Well, there are worse reasons.

She certainly pipped me at the post for early political awareness. Despite growing up in Edward Heath's constituency, my main perception of his importance was that he opened my brother's grammar school fete. Otherwise, my childhood recollection of politics was a playground skipping rhyme, each girl stepping into the turning rope as her name was called:

"Vote, vote, vote for little Debbie,
Calling Debbie at the door,
For Debbie is a lady
And she's going to have a baby
So we won't vote for Debbie any more.
CHUCK HER OUT!"

To our way of thinking, this dismissal seemed only fair. Astonishing, then, that the Prime Minister to emerge from first election in which my generation was old enough to vote was a lady by the name of Margaret. It seems like ancient history now.

Young Runners

July/August 2010

We did it – and we've got the medals to prove it!

My seven-year-old daughter Laura asked me last summer whether she could join me on a Race for Life, the 5km fun run in aid of Cancer Research. These runs are held all over the country, and I've run one every summer since Laura was born. There are many venues. At Lydiard Park in Swindon I ran through mud in pouring rain. On the runways of Kemble Airfield there was a cold fog, and I kept my fingers crossed that someone had warned air traffic control. But on Clifton Down in Bristol, there's always scorching sunshine, and I have to pour my water bottle over my head to keep cool.

So I was delighted when Laura showed an interest in taking part, and not only because it would provide a good excuse if my finishing time was a bit slow.

We did a little bit of preparation. Hearing the bell ring while we were still half way to school, Laura would break into a trot and pipe up, "This is good training".

Even more important than training is making sure you have a pink race outfit. (Well, this is a women's only event.) For any man standing on Clifton Down on Race Day, it must be intimidating to see ten thousand pink clad women converging purposefully on the starting line. It's like a very camp episode of Doctor Who – the Pinkonauts, though not quite as scary as a 10k race I did, pre-Laura, at the Moreton-in-Marsh Fire Services Training College. That route included startlingly realistic plane crashes, train derailments, motorway pile-ups and burned-out office blocks. Running that race was like fleeing from a holocaust. I'm sure the dramatic scenery triggered an adrenalin rush, so we all finished that bit faster.

One other key point on the Race for Life dress code is that every runner puts a pink sign on her back by way of a dedication. This makes for an emotional run. You oscillate from hope to despair and back again, running behind "Me! I survived!", "Dad, who lost his brave battle", "My five-year-old son, now fully recovered". For a little while we ran behind someone who had her mother's dates on her back, as on a tombstone, and I realised with a start that she had died the day before the race. Yet knowing we were raising so much money, that we were united, that we all cared so, so much, made it on balance a life-enhancing uplifting occasion. Girlpower, indeed.

But as with any race, there are those who treat it first and foremost as a competition. Laura was initially disappointed to learn that I'd never actually won a Race for Life, but I thought she'd taken on board my explanation that taking part and raising money for Cancer Research was the point until half way round she declared, "You know, Mummy, I don't think we're going to win."

5km is a long way when you're seven, and for the second half of the run, it took a bribe of a Love Heart every half kilometre to lure her to the end. I was proud that she rose to the occasion and managed to produce a dramatic sprint for the last few hundred metres. We crossed the line hand-in-hand, beaming broadly – we definitely earned our medals, and I was as proud as she was. I wore mine to the supermarket that afternoon. And as for the pink goody bags – well, as the sponsor likes to say, every little helps.

Laura's Fishing Tips

September 2010

Checking my archive, it appears I was away on holiday when the September issue was being prepared, so did not contribute. Instead the ominous line "Debbie Young is away" appeared in this issue – the only time in my six years as a columnist. Out of curiosity, I checked on my blog to see exactly what was keeping me from my duties, and discovered we were in Inverness on our summer holiday. For the sake of continuity, rather than leave this month blank here, I'm adding a post inspired by that trip.

A walk along the banks of the River Ness suggests my seven-year-old daughter Laura might be destined for a scientific career.

"Why does the ground stay there and not get washed away by the water in the river?" she asks me.

Cue for some improvised theorising, concocted by the very unscientific me, drawing on vague memories of a documentary about soil erosion and news stories about flooding.

Strolling further along the riverbank, we pause opposite the lay-by where fisherman park their cars. They cluster together, comparing notes, planning strategy. It's clearly a very serious sport around here.

We see several cyclists arrive, perilously dangling their fully extended fishing rods behind them, and hope they won't hook any passing pedestrians. We watch them don thigh-high waders before they trudge through the fast-moving shallows to cast their rods into deeper waters.

"Don't the fish notice them?" queries Laura.

I fail to dredge up any memories from school biology lessons about the fish's field of vision.

"Maybe fishing rods are always brown or green or grey so that fish will think they're just tree branches hanging over the river," I suggest. "After all, you never see fishermen with brightly coloured fishing rods. And they tie things called flies on to their hooks – bits of feather and suchlike that are meant to look like naturally occurring river insects that fish usually eat."

Laura considers this proposition.

"Then I think they should stick leaves on their rods, too, to make them look more like branches. Otherwise I'm surprised that the fish fall for it."

I was wondering why we'd never seen the fisherman catch anything.

The Centre of the World

October 2010

"Why isn't our village mentioned on television more often?" asks my small daughter, Laura, as we're watching the weather forecast. "They mention Bristol all the time."

The swooping BBC weather map has just reached the city where her grandparents live. Our airspace, as ever, they have passed over without a mention.

For Laura, rural Gloucestershire is the centre of the world. Now and again she seeks my reassurance that we will live here forever. She worries that I may sell the house. When I gently suggest that she may one day want to move away to university, or in pursuit of a career or a husband, she gives me an old-fashioned look.

I understand. I still feel a gravitational pull towards my own roots in London suburbia. I was born not far from the Greenwich Meridian, by which the whole world set its clocks – proof, to my childish mind, that I lived at the centre of the world. Any mention on the telly of Sidcup still makes me feel proprietorial, even though it's likely to be in the context of a comedy show – *Porridge* and *Rab C Nesbitt* both used Sidcup to raise an easy laugh.

In my subconscious there lies a world map. A large pin marks Sidcup as the focal point. Radiating out, in pastel colours, are the territories I've explored, while large tracts of uncharted land remain dark. Even today I take pleasure in visiting places I've never been, so that I can mentally colour them in. My map looks pretty colourful these days, but Sidcup's central pin remains in place.

Few people feel no pull towards their roots. We are all like tethered goats, though some have longer ropes. My Scottish husband, an economic migrant to England at the age of 20, has lived and worked in many English towns and travelled as far India for holidays, but every summer he heads north, as compelled as a homing swallow, to conquer another few Munros (Scottish mountains over 3,000 feet high). Avidly he records his conquests on a vast mountain map that fills our kitchen table. If Laura had been a boy, he'd have insisted on naming her Munro. Both she and I are very glad she is a girl.

About the time I was busy being born in Sidcup, a Tetbury-born friend of mine left home for university. His career took him all over the country before he eventually settled in Norfolk – about as far east of his roots as he could get without leaving England. Yet in retirement, what should be at the centre of his thoughts but the area in which he was raised? He's now penning a series of whimsical stories, based on the tiny territory of his boyhood, meticulously remembering every hill, every field and every lane.

Laura's personal map is already of conquistadorial proportions: not many seven-year-olds have travelled as widely. Before she was four, she'd been to Albania; her first kiss, at the age of three, was from a small Greek boy in Athens. This summer she added the Outer Hebrides to her empire. She's now set her sights on Mexico.

"How many countries are there in the world, Mummy?" she asked the other day, wondering how many she has yet to visit.

"One hundred and ninety-four," advised the Internet.

"And which one is the most popular?"

For a moment I'm stumped, till I consider a democratic approach.

"If you asked everyone in the world, the most votes would probably go to China," I suggest.

She frowned disapproval, patting her "Team England" t-shirt to indicate where she'd cast hers. (Later, doing the laundry, I check where her t-shirt was made. No prizes for guessing its country of origin. I decide I'd better not tell her.)

But no matter how far Laura travels, I'm sure her rural Gloucestershire home will always be her favourite destination. And now, as the autumn nights start to draw in, we are both very happy to be here.

Clear the Decks with Boughs of Holly

November 2010

The pre-Christmas clear-out is well underway in our household.

"If you don't get rid of the old toys that you've grown out of, there'll be no room for any Christmas presents," I warn my seven-year-old daughter.

Unlike her more capitalistic cousin Tim, Laura can't be persuaded to sell her old toys for a profit. Car boot sales leave her cold. She forms strong attachments to her cuddly toys: each has a name and a personality. Even I find myself drawn to the livelier characters: Candyfloss, the comical greying white poodle; its close friend and straight man, Butlin the spotty dog; Poonia and Pink, the fanciful unicorns; Sweetie, the soft-bodied baby doll who calls me Grandma. Laura would no sooner sell her dolls than sell her family. No doubt I'll find this a comfort when I'm old.

When the Toytown clutter gets too much for me, I entertain a shamefully ungrateful fantasy: that my house gets burnt to the ground. The conflagration is colourful as a

Christmas tree. Well, it should be, with all those plastic toys as fuel. We then set up home in a minimalistic Ikea showroom, our possessions stowed invisibly in storage baskets arranged on bookcases called Billy. But oh, the flat-packs! When I think of all that self-assembly, the current muddle doesn't seem so bad.

Killing time before a medical appointment, I wander round a toyshop. Don't shop until you've dropped, I remind myself, eyeing the Barbies and board games, both of which we already have plenty, thank you very much.

"Drop a few big bags of toys into one of the many charity shops while she's at school," a little voice tells me. "She'll never notice that they're gone."

I'm not convinced.

And so on to plan B: we could give her only very tiny toys as presents this Christmas. Then space would not be an issue. My husband, studying for a geology degree, has just acquired a microscope.

"Maybe she'd like to start an atom collection," I wonder.

The trouble is, things are just too cheap these days. It would be easier to resist buying large toys if they cost more. How much more sensible it would be if toys were priced according to volume. The huge wooden rocking-horse, lovingly carved by Laura's grandpa, would then be priceless. It all makes perfect sense. I have a similar proposal for calorie distribution: a square of chocolate should contain a fraction of the calories of a Ryvita.

But then a smarter strategy occurs to me: we'll tackle the problem from the other end. There are two small but serviceable cellars beneath our cottage. And they are empty.

"How do you fancy a playroom for Christmas?" I suggest. "We can convert one of the cellars as your present."

"A playroom!" Her eyes light up. "I've always wanted a playroom."

"A playroom. A music room. A disco. We can make it whatever you like."

"Oh, yes please, Mummy!"

Problem solved. And at a bargain price, too.

Now all we have to do is to work out how to gift-wrap it.

Let It Glow

December 2010/January 2011

You don't need me to tell you that the autumn colours have been fantastic this year. Each day in late October, early November, I kept thinking *I really must bring my camera with me next time I'm out.* Everywhere I went, breathtaking treescapes of gold, amber and bronze, dramatic as fireworks, rose out of rich, dark newly-ploughed hills.

Then, overnight, they disappeared. Strong winds stripped the trees bare, leaving muddy heaps of compost at their feet. It was as if a herbicidal maniac had been on the rampage. Suddenly it was winter. The clocks had gone back. And it was dark.

My sense of loss at this overnight tragedy made me less dismissive than I might otherwise have been when a day or two later I spotted my first Christmas tree of the year in the front window of a house near my mum's. Not only had the occupants put the tree up on the wrong side of Remembrance Day, they'd also sprayed lavish drifts of fake snow on their windowpanes, as if egging on the winter to do its worst. The shiny red stars and golden bells were a garish echo of the subtle russets and auburns of the departed autumn leaves, but boy, was it a cheery sight.

All at once I found myself looking forward to the rash of Christmas lights that would inevitably follow. Nothing cheers me in winter as much as bright lights – in a former life I must have been a Druid. For the rest of the year, my usual mantra is "Put that light out!" (so maybe I was once an ARP warden). My husband and daughter treat our household like a Christmas tree all year round in terms of lighting, and for the rest of the year, I go round turning unnecessary lights off, muttering disapproval. But when it comes to midwinter, I need a burst of light to stop me hibernating.

Certain local routes round here provide a real tonic at this season. Last year, the white-lit Christmas trees, hung proudly like flags above the shops through the centre of Tetbury, were as cheering to me as any Olympic opening ceremony. And who can resist the uplifting annual switching on of the Christmas lights? Passing by the Arboretum, I'll slow down to savour the "shop window" for the Enchanted Wood, which revitalises bare trees with coloured floodlights. And just a little further down the Bath Road, there's an ever-growing beacon that takes many by surprise. The first time I passed that way after dark, I was convinced that I was about to come across a major conflagration on the road ahead. I listened out for sirens, but there were none. Rounding the bend, I discovered it was actually just Willesley's cattery and kennels in all their electric glory. Their furry residents must feel ever so festive by Christmas Day.

In the past, I've shied away from too lavish a Christmas lighting scheme at my own home. Think Ikea candle arches, and you'll get the picture. But this year, in the depths of this dark winter, I feel the need to throw caution to the winds, which is appropriate enough as my electricity comes from the wind-powered Ecotricity in Stroud. If their profits suddenly go up next quarter, you'll know the reason why: I'm planning to splash out this year on the festive lighting front. Now, can anyone tell me the best place in Tetbury to buy an illuminated reindeer?

Wishing all *Tetbury Advertiser* readers a very merry Christmas, and a New Year filled with light. Let it glow, let it glow, let it glow...

How to Get to the Bottom of the Ironing Basket

February 2011

The ironing board is on the landing. This may seem an odd place to keep it, but it's solving a long-standing problem: the apparently bottomless ironing basket.

It's not that I dislike ironing: in the right frame of mind, I find it very soothing. Research shows that repetitive tasks provide similar benefits to meditation – knitting and jogging also qualify. But lately the view from my utility room of a dreary browning post-snow garden has deterred me from taking up my position at the ironing board. And the distinctive aroma of over-wintering guinea pig, which decamped to the adjacent worktop during the cold snap, is a further disincentive.

As I hovered in the utility room the day before spring term began, trying to summon up the energy to tackle a week's worth of school uniforms, an inspiration flashed into my head. For this I must thank the author Susan Hill. At Tetbury's Yellow-Lighted Bookshop's wonderful Book

Festival last summer, she talked about her latest book *Howard's End is on the Landing* which describes the year she spent rereading books stashed around her house.

Like her, I have many books on my landing, which my husband recently redecorated. I took the opportunity to reorganise the bookshelves, showing the contents off to best advantage. Now at the top are decades of diaries, the earliest dating from when I was eight. Below are displayed precious and obscure books from my childhood (anyone else remember *Torchy the Battery Boy?*), through to the bittersweet teenage comforters such as Dodie Smith's *I Capture the Castle*. Next come the dog-eared favourites from my university days. Well, some are less dog-eared than others: one day I really will read all four volumes of Richardson's *Clarissa*, bought at vast expense in a wild moment of undergraduate optimism. Then there's the vast collection of hobby-related guides acquired in my leisure-rich child-free days. These haven't seen much action since I acquired a child, whose own bedroom is now bursting at the seams with books.

I never tire of looking at my bookshelves, and the display on the landing will be a lovely backdrop to my ironing. The location offers other conveniences: a thick, warm Indian rug under foot; the adjoining bathroom where

I can easily top up the iron's water chamber; nearby wardrobes for immediately hanging up the ironed clothes (far better than turning the kitchen into a holding bay). I'm convinced that on the landing, I'll make great headway through the ironing basket – at least as long as I can ignore the comfy rocking chair in the corner, an ideal place to curl up with a book.

But for now I'm determined that this refreshing change of scene will restore momentum to the task in hand. What's more, I'm thinking of applying the same principle to other stalled proceedings. So once I've finished typing this, I'm off to do my tax return in the bath. Must press on...

Spring Fever

March 2011

It's no wonder it is called Spring. All of a sudden things are springing up out of nowhere, as if someone's put nature on fast forward without telling me.

How come I never noticed the snowdrops until they were in flower? They can't have appeared overnight, fully formed. And did those daffodil shoots, now four inches high in my front garden, really pop up like a jack-in-the-box the minute my back was turned?

It's not just flowers that have been miraculously materialising. When I took my daughter to her tap-dancing class yesterday afternoon, two sisters in her class had gained a baby brother since last week – and I hadn't even noticed that their mother was pregnant. It's bad enough that the weekly tap-dancing classes seem to take place every other day. To miss a whole human gestation period is beyond the pale.

At this rate, I had better make sure I get out and about in the next few days, or before I know it the wild garlic and primroses will have come and gone. Those unlikely roadside bedfellows are my favourite signs of spring; I'd hate to miss my annual treat of driving down the country lanes with open windows, invigorated by the pungent air. And I can't get by without seeing that gorgeous blue carpet that will be unrolling in local woodlands any day now. The delicate scent transports me back to the spring of my childhood, when no classroom was complete without a jam jar crammed with bluebells on every windowsill. It doesn't make sense to me that in the days when we were all allowed to pick them to our hearts content, there was never any shortage of wild flowers.

Blink, and I'll miss the violet haze of flax that briefly rests, gossamer-like, over too few fields round here. It's such a welcome respite from the garish, choking rape that seems to take over the countryside for a few weeks each spring, like a horrible bully that wants everything its own way.

In no time at all I'll be wondering whether I'm too late to admire the sumptuous pinks and mauves of the Arboretum's rhododendrons. Nor do I want to miss the spindly-legged lambs skittering about fields that were once home only to sluggish, chubby sheep. All too soon they'll have turned into sturdy teenagers, waiting their turn to go to market.

The trouble is, when you live in an area like this all year round, it's easy not to notice what tourists travel miles to see. If your chief shopping destination is the Co-op rather than the Highgrove shop, and your shopping list is for groceries rather than rare antiques, you're bound to have a different perspective on the local landscape.

So when are they going to mend all these potholes?

Keeping Up with My Sporty Daughter

April 2011

"What's your favourite sport, Mummy?" asks my small daughter on the way to Brownies.

I rack my brains, trying to think of which sports I can actually claim I do.

"Running," I reply, from my list of one.

"What about badminton? Or football? Or tag rugby? Or tennis?"

She reels off some of the many activities she's tried at school since moving up to the Juniors in September. At the small village primary school that she attends, her class has a PE rota, enabling the children to sample a different sport for three weeks at a time.

Her after-school schedule is equally varied. In the last couple of years, she's tried ballet, tap, modern, country dancing, street dance, karate and gym. With a trampoline *de rigueur* in every modern child's garden, she does quite a lot of random bouncing, too. Then there's roller-skating at the leisure centre on Saturday nights with friends, swimming with Daddy at whichever local pool currently has the warmest water, and ice-skating whenever we encounter a rink. (She's skated outdoors in Paris and Amsterdam so far.)

On this evidence, I don't believe the newspaper hype that our children are growing up fat and unfit – not round here, at least, where we have so many open, safe places for them to play.

My childhood experience of sport was very different. For baby-boomers like me, PE in the Infants meant pretending to be a tree to the sounds of "Music and Movement" on the radio and learning to do bunny hops over benches. In the Juniors, my only real sporting memory is of the obstacle race on Sports Day, even though in the first year we were lucky enough to have a former national athlete as our class teacher. Mrs Stocking, formerly Patricia Kippax, had sprinted in the 1964 Tokyo Olympics, and a few years later, there she was, letting us chase her round the school field, much to the amusement of other staff.

At secondary school, the PE teachers were only interested in the naturally talented few who might make county standard. My best friend and I jogged round chatting at the back on our cross-country runs past the graveyard, trying to conceal American Tan tights kept on for warmth beneath our hockey socks. In the hockey season, I'd always volunteer to be goalie as I reckoned it might require the least physical movement.

Whenever the Olympics came around, the events were so alien to me that they might just as well have been on Mars. I did recognise I was witnessing history being made as the American swimmer Mark Spitz secured his seventh gold medal at the 1972 Munich Olympics, but only because my teenage sister had a crush on him and made me watch.

But next year, when the Olympics come to London, to my daughter, as for so many other local children, the sports will seem real and tangible, because she will already have tried out so many of them. She's won a few medals herself for sporting activities, for reaching a certain stage in her gym club and for completing some sponsored walks and runs. She will watch the games as a fellow sportswoman, seeing herself as a contender.

And I bet when hockey comes up on her rota next autumn, she won't be keeping her tights on.

Tattoo or Not to Tattoo? That is the Question

May 2011

Unleashed from their hibernation by the recent summery weather, tattoos are appearing all around us. Even in the famously stylish Cotswolds, I can guarantee you'll find one on a white shoulder near you. And even when that shoulder is sun-burnished to hot pink, the dark, brooding tones of the tattoo will still shine through.

Tattoos are constantly taking me by surprise. The most unlikely people have been showing me their latest acquisitions. On occasion it's been as surprising as discovering that a polar bear has black skin – one of the many fascinating facts I've learned this term from my daughter's school topic, "Pole to Pole".

Taking a dip in a local public swimming pool, I was alarmed to discover that I was the only adult uniformly flesh-coloured. Surreptitiously surveying the other swimmers, I began to feel as undressed as if I'd forgotten my swimsuit. Even the children were not unblemished, thanks to the invention of the (mercifully) temporary tattoo. The closest we had to these when I was a child was "transfers", all of which were small and square, and we'd buy them in great sheets from the paper shop for sixpence.

My small daughter Laura discovered temporary tattoos on holiday in Greece a few years ago, when she was three, and she spent a happy hour on the beach adorning her parents' lazy bodies with colourful little pictures. I've always liked tiny vehicles for art. I'm a long-term collector of enamel pin-badges and I love postage stamps: *Borrowers'* paintings in frilly frames, so at first I found the temporary tattoos not unappealing. Only that evening in a smart taverna did I realise that, to the uninformed observer, there is no discernible difference between the temporary and permanent kind of tattoo. The festoons of flowers adorning my husband's shoulders attracted some quizzical looks.

But at least we were on holiday so it didn't particularly matter. Not so lucky was our friend Ida, who at a dinner party succumbed to Laura's entreaty to put a tattoo on her forehead. The wine that had made this seem such a good idea at the time had lost its influence by the Monday morning, when she had to sit through an important business meeting, the tattoo still firmly in place. (Sellotape is the answer, by the way, should you ever find yourself in this position.)

I cannot imagine ever being prepared to commit to any one design for permanent adornment. There's no item of clothing or accessory that I'd wear day in, day out, so how do people choose tattoos? Ignoring the obvious foible of etching your current partner's name into your flesh ("current" being the significant word here), even a favourite motif might lose its appeal in time. Tinkerbell on a twenty-year-old's calf won't look quite the same on a sixty-year-old's.

It's not just the ageing process that takes its toll. I might once have thought a bee would be a time-proof emblem for me. My name is Hebrew for bee, and I am such a busy person that friends buy me bee-themed presents without knowing the significance of my name. But had I plumped for a bee tattoo in my youth, I'd have been heading straight for the lasers once Sarah Ferguson adopted it for her coat of arms as part of her metamorphosis into the Duchess of York. (I reckon that's why we see so few bees about these days – the supposed bee-killing virus is a myth, they're just all keeping a low profile out of embarrassment.) I'm very fond of daisies, and my bathroom is strewn with them in various forms, but I'd soon change my tune should

Kerry Katona bring out a "Daisy" perfume as part of her new, fresh, clean image. To avoid tattoo traps, you have to expect the unexpected.

But then in Tesco's the other day (always a fruitful place for the summertime tattoo-spotter), I caught sight of a truly timeless tattoo. A swan-like pair of angels' wings filled the bare flesh above a young mum's white strapless vest.

These will see me out, I can imagine her thinking in the tattoo parlour. *And I'll be all set for heaven when I get there.*

It's got to be the ultimate fashion statement.

Saying it with Trees

June 2011

So what did you like best about the royal wedding? For me, near the top of the list was the prayer penned jointly by the bride and groom. Like the confessional pledge made by Charles and Camilla at their ceremony, it was disarmingly candid and sincere. A touching testimony to the strength of their relationship, it was more impressive than any amount of pageantry.

But it wasn't the couple's eloquence that moved me the most. It was something far more surprising. Can you guess? I'll give you a clue: they were the tallest guests. They were welcomed by Kate's new father-in-law. And they'll soon be taking root at Highgrove.

Yes, I'm talking about the trees. Before we were allowed to see inside Westminster Abbey, Huw Edwards gave the floral decorations a big build-up, but trees? Totally unexpected, they took my breath away. It was startling to see their branches rising up, bringing life, youth and vigour to the ancient stone edifice. They softened the vast heights of the Abbey roof, while symbolising shelter from the elements and adversity. For the young couple they alluded to the promise of future growth and life far beyond the ceremony of the day. I wondered whether their leaves were rustling in anticipation as warm air rose from the excited mass of illustrious guests below.

Yet what more natural a decoration for the wedding of a country boy raised in rural Gloucestershire, a stone's throw from our National Arboretum, the magnificent Highgrove Gardens his childhood back yard? I've twice toured the grounds at Highgrove and each time they have struck me as a wonderful place to grow up, and not only for the spectacular treehouse. Remarkable features pepper the place as you move from one garden room to another, from the amusing black and white garden to the colourful potager, from the fragrant thyme walk to open meadow views. I particularly adore the stumpery, where spent trees gain new dignity. (At Highgrove, old trees never die – Prince Charles just finds another use for them.)

So the wedding trees will now be planted at Highgrove, where they will bring a tear to the eye of many a future garden visitor. As the years go by, tourists will marvel at how much the trees have grown. Maybe in time royal offspring will be photographed playing beneath them. Rather more accessible to general public view will be the new wedding cake tree, rather sweetly planted in the churchyard of St Mary's by the Duchess of Cornwall for the local WI of which she is pleasingly a member.

I predict that tree nurseries nationwide will now experience a boom in sales, thanks to Will and Kate's inspired idea. Engaged couples everywhere will be adding saplings to their guest list. No wedding will be complete without a tree or two in the congregation. If I were in charge of wedding bookings at Westonbirt Arboretum, I'd be rubbing my hands together with glee, pound signs ringing up in my eyes: where better to hold a local tree-themed wedding?

Mind you, I hope that the trees don't completely supplant flowers in the wedding ceremony. If they do, one popular custom will surely disappear: the throwing of the bridal bouquet over the shoulder, to be caught by single girls wishing to be the next to marry. Tossing the caber may be fun to watch, but there aren't many girls who'd want to catch one.

How to Pack for the Summer Holidays

July/August 2011

Packing. The very thought of it takes the edge off the excitement of going on holiday, at least till we're on our way.

It shouldn't be such a difficult task. As we spend most holidays in our camper van, we don't have to bother with suitcases. We pack our possessions straight into the van's streamlined cupboards, and here they stay, out of sight, until we need them. Well, that's the theory, anyway.

Years ago, when we were child-free, holidays meant sailing in Greece. Packing in those days meant shoehorning toy-sized toiletries and capsule wardrobes into a collapsible sausage-shaped bag, ready for decanting into ship's lockers on arrival. A camera, notebook and pen (plus daily access to yesterday's English newspaper for my husband) were our only desert-island luxuries. Leaving behind the clutter of everyday life at home and at work was exhilarating. Forget Feng Shui – there were barely any material items to arrange.

Then in time, we had a baby to pack too. Until babies are about three, there's an inverse relationship between the size of the child and the volume of luggage it requires. Just as Laura's own baggage was starting to reduce – no more bottles, bibs or buggies – she hit toddlerhood, when she didn't want to be confined to a boat. She needed playparks full of children to become her new friends. Any nationality, language no object, provided the children were her size.

And so slickly we transferred, like *Chitty Chitty Bang Bang*, onto land. We traded in our boat for a camper van. Drier, less lurching, and less likely to strand us due to weather conditions, it was a welcome and natural evolution from amphibian to reptile. And while I was in charge of packing, it was still soothingly minimalist too.

But now that Laura packs her own bags for holidays, new challenges have arisen. Numerous cuddly toys and dolls anthropomorphise into inseparable friends who would simply pine away if left at home without her. By the end of last year's summer holiday, Laura's entourage took over the entire vehicle. So for our half-term trip to the Highlands, I decide to set a new rule: one bag of toys per person. A serious constraint for Gadget Man, but a less daunting challenge for me: most of my toys are books to read or write in. It is easy to smuggle extra rations onto the van's built-in bookshelf.

I expect a rebellion before our departure. But no, Laura sits demurely on her booster seat with an old black barrel handbag of mine bulging at her side. On her lap is a single cuddly toy: Heather the Best-Dressed Rabbit. (Heather even has her own gas-mask case for this term's World War II topic). I've suggested that instead of taking lots of toys, Laura pack a bag of Heather's clothes to ring the changes along the way. I am pleasantly startled to see she's taken my advice.

Pointing the van north, we hit the road. The half-grown crops in the Cotswold fields undulate as we pass, as if waving goodbye. They will seem so soft and green on our return from serious Scottish mountains.

Four hours later, when we stop for the night at Morecambe Bay, the true contents of the little black bag are revealed. With a coy, self-satisfied smile, Laura unzips it and begins to pull out an endless stream of toys. It's like watching a conjuror do the handkerchief trick. Three rag dolls, four horses, two dogs, a bird...all these and more are soon strewn around the camper van, leaving my husband and I scrabbling, as ever, for a space big enough to sit in. One bag of toys it is, so I cannot complain. But what an astonishing mastery of the art of packing for one so young. I sigh and sit down next to Heather. When the summer holidays come round, I think I'll put Laura in charge of loading the van.

Back to School

September 2011

As you will have noticed if you have been anywhere near a supermarket since June, this month it's back to school, and for primary school children like my eight-year-old daughter Laura, another term means another topic.

When I was that age, a topic was a simple self-driven task: four sheets of paper to fill on a specific subject, the next on the list set by the teacher. I can see now that these topics were time-fillers, to occupy the brighter pupils who had completed all the work cards while the others caught up. I remember vividly picking bits of pebbledash off my suburban semi-detached house to Sellotape on to my rather literal interpretation of the topic "My Home".

These days, it's not so simple. The modern topic is a whole-class cross-curricular activity in which a single theme unites the many subjects to be taught throughout the term. Picture the topic, a spider at the heart of its web, the focal point of many subject strands woven cleverly together. The whole is definitely much greater than the sum of the parts;

the result is a fun learning experience, leading to a broad, balanced outlook on life that I wish I'd had at Laura's age (or, indeed, now).

Last term, for example, Laura's topic was World War II. I was astonished at how dextrously this sombre subject was presented to capture her young imagination – and capture her imagination it certainly did. The class didn't want the term to end.

"I think this is probably the best topic I'll ever do in my life, Mummy," she declared at half term.

Digging for victory in the school's new vegetable garden and comparing the effectiveness of different materials for black-out ticked the science box. Writing speeches for Churchill, composing propaganda slogans and drafting newspaper reports covered literacy. Calculating the best use of their sweet ration was about as compelling a numeracy task as you can get. Swing dance was a popular PE session, and learning catchy war-time songs went down well for music. One of Laura's friends spent most of a playdate at our house singing "We'll be hanging out the washing on the Siegfried Line" at the top of her voice, with as much enthusiasm as she'd sing any pop song. I'm not sure what part of the National Curriculum was served by the children sitting under their desks for half hour for a mock air raid, but it's certainly a lesson they will remember for the rest of their lives.

Ever the dutiful parent, I conscripted my parents to visit Laura's class to talk about their experiences as evacuees from London, my father having been helpfully sent to the Cotswolds. Indeed, his wartime love affair with the area (and one Dorothy Duckett) is what led me to live here myself. He brought his own children back for summer holidays, and I vividly remember deciding when I was about Laura's age that this was where I would live when I grew up.

To give some airtime to all sides, I also invited an elderly German friend, contemporary with my parents, to write the class a letter about her own experiences of evacuation to the German countryside. Many of her neighbours were killed in British air raids, and she has suffered from claustrophobia ever since her numerous trips to the air raid shelter. An old Dutch school friend of mine recounted his mother's experience of Nazi occupied Holland. Her greatest trauma was losing her mother and her home to an American (yes, an American) bomb. Friendly fire: it happened then too.

But just when I think the World War II topic has drawn to a close, while packing for our summer holidays I'm taken aback by Laura's request to divert the itinerary. She thinks our leisurely tour of France in our camper van should now wander east: she wants us to annex Germany. I'd be less keen to change our plans had I not overheard a game that she was playing with friends one afternoon towards the end of term. The trampoline had become a Nazi concentration camp, in which Laura and two of her friends were imprisoned.

A fourth friend was playing the role of a German soldier. Fetching some glasses of squash from the kitchen, she shouted at them, "Here, drink this slime, prisoners!"

In the interests of international relations, I think I'd better take Laura to Germany to make some German friends. But while we're there, I don't think I'll mention the war.

How to Make a Weather Forecast More Meaningful

October 2011

"Are pirates real, Mummy?" my daughter asks out of the blue one day.

As a child I lay awake in fear at night worrying about Captain Hook, so I'm anxious to allay her fears.

"No, darling, they're only in stories like *Peter Pan.*"

A few days later, the BBC Radio 4 lunchtime news scuppers my deception with a report of a pirate attack off the coast of Somalia. Laura looks at me accusingly.

"Oh, but they're not pirates like Captain Hook," I try to reassure her. "And there aren't any in this country, anyway."

The trouble lies in the terms of reference. To Laura, all pirates have wooden legs, parrots and hook hands, not motor launches and polybags of heroin.

The same problem crops up with the weather forecast. One morning the radio alarm wakes us up with a report about a tornado in Birmingham.

"But you told me we don't get tornados in this country!"

"Well, not big ones, like the one in *The Wizard of Oz*," I explain. "In Birmingham, there won't have been any cattle swept up into the sky or barns blown flat – it will just have seemed a bit windy."

Despite my attempt at reassurance, Laura is on the lookout for flying houses all day.

These national reporters of news and weather have a lot to answer for. They bandy about terms that may make good radio, but which mean very little to us normal human beings. And when they do come up with a clear, evocative description – such as the infamous "barbecue summer" that the weathermen have been promising us these last two years – their promises usually turn out to be false. (Or maybe weather forecasters like barbecuing on cold rainy days. I suppose it would minimise the risk of starting a forest fire.)

So for this autumn I've formulated some new definitions that are much more meaningful to those of us living in the Cotswolds. Not for me the Richter scale of earthquakes (I was disappointed to find that a friend experiencing a 4.5 reported in Amsterdam did not feel the earth move) nor the anthropomorphising of hurricanes. Calling the latest one Irene did nothing to make her more amendable to my American friends, stockpiling groceries and bottled water in their cellars. No, I'll be using terms of reference that relate directly to what I see when I look out of my cottage window.

First, there's the Tetbury Wind Scale. Force 1: autumn leaves are becalmed on trees. Force 2: a breeze flaps them about a bit. Force 3: the leaves depart the tree before their time. Force 4: twigs are blown down too. Force 5: look out! Bigger sticks are falling from the sky. Force 6: wind enough to fell a whole branch. Force 7: and the rest of the tree as well – beware of them on the roads as you drive to work. Force 8: Uh oh! Westonbirt Arboretum's had to close while they make it safe – but there could be some nice carved wooden souvenirs on sale next summer.

Then there's the Gloucestershire Snow Scale. Force 1 and we all just think how pretty it is, especially on the fields and trees. Force 2: we can still go about our daily business provided we take it slowly. By Force 4, only the 4x4s can make it through the lanes. Force 8 and you'll need to find a friendly farmer and borrow his tractor.

And then there's my Cotswold Drystone Wall weather gauge. Force 1 means you'll spot the odd little trickle of tiny stones after a mild frost, whereas Force 8 is an avalanche: whole walls tumbling down either side of every main road.

This in turn is a harbinger of a spring spent admiring the day-to-day progress of the skilled and hardy stone wallers repairing it as you drive to work.

I just hope it's not going to be another Pothole Winter.

Flu Jab Jeopardy – It's an Old Wives' Game

November 2011

Driving along the A433, I inadvertently accelerate every time I sneeze then reproach myself that it's impossible to catch flu from an influenza vaccine. My best friend, a pharmacist, told me so. But my aching left arm reminds me that in the few hours since I had my jab, I've started to feel distinctly unwell.

This morning's trip to the doctor's surgery should have made me feel a lot better. I was by far the healthiest person in the surgery and I brought the average age down by at least ten years. But now I'm sneezing for all I'm worth.

As my car kangaroos towards Willesley, I decide to take my mind off my symptoms by listening to the radio. I switch on to hear DJ Steve Wright baiting BBC Radio 2's resident doctor.

"So what you're saying, Doc, is that you really can catch a cold by being cold? Are you saying my mum was right when she told me I'd catch my death of cold for going out without a scarf?"

"Yes, she was."

"But this time last year, you told me that was an old wives' tale and I shouldn't believe it?"

You can almost hear Dr Hilary gritting his teeth. He is not enjoying this retraction.

"Ah, but there's been new research. It clearly shows that if you are cold, your immune system is suppressed. And therefore you're more likely to catch a cold."

It's an astonishing admission. This time next year, perhaps he'll be telling us you can catch flu from the vaccine – or that my mother was right when she said that if I leave the house with wet hair, I'll get pneumonia. If these urban myths are overturned, who knows what other old wives' tales will be proven true?

Goodness knows, there are plenty to choose from. Some I will never believe, but still can't help following. Even in the playground, I didn't for a moment accept that cutting your hand between your thumb and your forefinger would give you lockjaw. Nor did I really think that if you swallowed chewing gum, it would get wrapped around your heart. But I choose not to take either risk.

I was less convinced by my grandmother's insistence that if you don't eat beetroot, you'll never have good blood. Unfortunate experiences with a bullying dinner lady at infants' school left me forever unable to eat that lurid vegetable, regardless of the health implications.

I didn't want to believe my other grandmother's assertion that if you look in the mirror too long, you'll see the devil looking over your shoulder (presumably designed to nip vanity in the bud at an early age). But I still can't gaze in a mirror for too long without casting an anxious glance backwards – even the rear view mirror in my car. And killing spiders is a thing of the past in our household, thanks to my elderly neighbour's mantra: "If you want to live and thrive, let the spider keep alive". Should I be reckless enough to flatten one, I'd half expect a posse of spider mafia to turn up to get their revenge.

And now, thanks to Dr Hilary, I'm going to let myself be governed by another old wives' tale. I turn off the car radio and turn on the heater instead.

When It Comes to Christmas Presents, Small is Beautiful

December 2011/January 2012

'Tis the season to start tidying!

In the Young household, the arrival of the Advent calendar kicks off our annual quest to banish clutter. When Santa arrives, we don't want to have to tell him there's no room for new toys – or so I keep telling my daughter, Laura.

Not that we're anticipating a flurry of extravagant gifts this year. Now approaching her ninth festive season, Laura has produced a positively frugal letter to Santa, reflecting our current economic climate. Even if he delivers everything on her Christmas list, it won't take up much space. The intriguingly specific "yellow and white doggy key-ring" and "a biro with different colours" should fit easily in her pocket, while the requested "air freshener" will require only a couple of square inches of shelf space.

While I applaud my daughter's restraint, I'm anxious that she doesn't miss out on the most important Christmas present of all: a large cardboard box to play in for the rest of the holidays. (They don't call it Boxing Day for nothing.) A few weeks ago I invested in a big wooden ottoman for my bedroom. The even bigger cardboard outer in which it was packaged has since provided Laura with many happy hours of creative play. First of all it was a bus, taking her cuddly toys on outings. Then, as easily as *Chitty Chitty Bang Bang*, it turned amphibious, morphing first into a rowing boat then into a sailing ship. With the children from next door as stowaways, she spent a happy Saturday sailing round the living room. You don't need to live in the Lake District to beat *Swallows and Amazons* at their own game.

Laura's pocket-sized presents are the antidote to the huge items on my husband's wish-list. After a pleasant hour of Googling, "a large telescope with stand" is soon joined by "a powerful SLR camera", without which, it seems, no serious telescope is complete. At least I won't have to find house-room for these gifts, because he's also desirous of "a garden observatory" in which to use them. I'd like to see the postman fit that through our letterbox.

To be honest, I'm now at an age when I neither need nor covet Christmas presents. I'd be happier to have none at all. For me, as an atheist, the festive season is all about spending quality time with family and friends, and I'm planning my December social calendar like a military campaign. Though to my mind there's no finer place than Gloucestershire to spend Christmas, our festive tour of duty will take us as far afield as Scotland to ensure we can catch up with all those we love best. The only disadvantage is that after this holiday, I think I'll need another one to recover. Alternatively I could just go AWOL now and again to escape the action, unless Santa brings me the one thing featured on my Christmas wish-list: a cloak of invisibility.

Happy Christmas, everyone!

Tuning Grandma's Piano

(The Antidote to Chopsticks)

February 2012

The only thing worse than hearing 'Chopsticks' played repeatedly on the piano is hearing 'Chopsticks' played repeatedly on a piano that is badly out of tune.

At the turn of the year, my daughter acquires this party trick from a school friend who has learned it from her cousin over Christmas. 'Chopsticks' spreads like a virus among children. There can be few who are naturally immune. Roll on the day when the MMR vaccine gives way to the MMRC – Mumps, Measles, Rubella and Chopsticks.

But as this vaccination has yet to be invented, I decide the most effective remedy for my household is to get my piano tuned. My previous tuner in Bristol having retired, I scour the Internet in hope of finding a new one closer to home. To my amazement, I discover there's one in Didmarton – virtually on my doorstep. A phone call later he's literally on my doorstep, tool bag in hand.

Clearing the photos and other debris from the top of the piano, I explain to him the history of my particular instrument. As I do, I realise why I've been so tardy in getting it tuned: I'm worried that it's now beyond redemption and will have to be written off. A humble "cottage upright", it's not a valuable instrument, but it is precious to me.

Exactly 100 years old, it belonged to my beloved grandmother, who was born in 1900. Her stepfather bought it for her when she was about eight – the age my daughter is now. In her twenties, she took it to her new marital home in Sidcup. (I can still picture the piano in the corner of her dining room, family photos and trinkets on the top, and I often dream that I'm back in that room having tea.)

Her husband, my grandfather, was a gifted musician too poor to afford a musical career, but music was always his passion, passed down the family line. Unfortunately his musical genes passed me by, but I did eventually gain the piano. It went first to my more talented cousin, whose skills soon outgrew the instrument's powers. A trained opera singer, she played this piano at my wedding reception.

That I have chosen the right piano tuner to revive this family heirloom soon becomes clear. He reveals that his mother was also born in 1900. When I tell him my daughter's name is Laura, he immediately begins to play the eponymous tune, which I've never come across before, declaring it to be his favourite. When she comes home from school, Laura will be thrilled.

Lovingly he coaxes the piano back into good order. He suppresses the squeaks that had lately haunted the pedals. He handcrafts wooden shafts that give new voice to keys that had turned dumb. In turn, little by little, he brings each note back to just where it should be in the scale.

And then comes the grand finale: that fabulous moment when he shows off his handiwork by playing pieces that test every note on the keyboard. It's the piano tuner's equivalent to the typist's quick brown fox jumping over the lazy dog.

Even if there is no cure for 'Chopsticks', this is a most effective antidote. Thank you, Mr Felton – and may there be many encores.

The Tetbury Advertiser *is a great place to find a piano tuner and many other friendly local service providers!*

My Kodak Moments

March 2012

When the purchase of a new computer this month prompted me to transfer the files across from my old one, I realised with a start just how many digital photos I had accumulated.

The advent of digital photography instilled in me the blithe hope that I'd banish the growing stack of shoeboxes stuffed full of ancient snaps, teetering in a corner of my study. These pictures witness not only my progress from birth to adulthood, but also the evolution of photographic technology over the last half century.

The earliest photos, of me as a baby, were taken on the family's old box-style Kodak, where you had to peer down into the top of the camera at a reflected image rather than holding it in front of you.

By the time I was old enough to master that camera myself, Instamatics had been invented. Chunky, detachable, flash cubes could be plugged into the top, rotating after each shot.

When I was about 30, the compact camera arrived on the scene. These made film changes easy. Instead of connecting a film to a spool inside the camera, you just dropped in a cartridge. Once the film was developed, the negatives came back in the same cartridge for easy storage.

I remember being buttonholed on a plane by an enthusiastic Kodak rep a few months before these cameras were launched: "Our new invention will change the course of photography for ever!" Famous last words: earlier this year, Kodak filed for bankruptcy protection, the pioneer of film-based photography vanquished by the digital age.

I got my first digital camera not long after the birth of my daughter Laura. Only the first year of her life is captured on traditional film, the rest is trapped inside my computer. Every time I open the My Photos file, I flinch, half closing my eyes to avoid recognising just how many there are. There are simply too many to manage. Of course, there is the handy facility to change the image names and sort them into useful folders – far better than writing on the back of a print with a biro – but does anyone exist who is really that organised? Certainly not in my household.

And yet with the thousands of photos that I have available at the touch of a button, apart from my wedding photos (taken by a fabulous local professional, Clint

Randall), I still only ever print and look at the few pictures that struck me at the moment of taking as instant classics. My favourites include an informal shot of my baby daughter and me taken at a party without our knowledge, the two of us laughing on top of a Welsh hill, and a cute shot at a farm park of Laura with a bunny on her lap.

But to be honest, the images I value most are not even in digital format: they exist only in my head. My grandma standing at her front door, laughing at a joke we'd shared just before I ran off to school; my daughter lying in her hospital cot the night after she was born (I stayed awake all night gazing at her, convinced she was the most beautiful thing I'd ever seen); my lovely old friend Joe, blowing kisses and waving as I left on the airport bus from New York's Grand Central Station for my journey home. As he receded in the distance, I willed that image to stay in my brain. If this was the last time I ever saw him, I mused, that would be a great way to remember him. I had no idea how prophetic that was: he died suddenly, unexpectedly, before I could see him again.

It's like the old saying that radio beats television because the pictures are better. Or maybe I'm just bad at photography. Perhaps in future I should leave it to the experts – and hope that my brain doesn't run out of storage space any time soon.

Another Term, Another Topic, Another School Trip

April 2012

These days, it seems a term does not go by without the children being taken on a school trip. This policy is especially valuable in these rural parts, where our children do not have as much opportunity to travel as their city-dwelling peers. I'm quietly envious every time Laura comes home clutching a permission slip for the current term's trip. I was raised in suburbia, and by the age of 12 I was regularly taking the 30 minute train ride into London to visit museums and parks at weekends. Not only did I travel without an adult, I also used to take my much younger cousins – unthinkable these days for reasons you don't need me to go into here. But we had very few school trips, and none at all in primary school.

Laura's school outings are carefully planned to enhance the term's topic, and the destination is not always obvious. I wondered where on earth would they go to study the Second World War. It emerged that for visiting schools, the Steam Museum at Swindon will recreate an "evacuee experience". I had a lump in my throat as I packed her off to school that day. She had to wear a 1930s frock and take a teddy, wear a gas mask box over her shoulder and have a luggage label bearing her name pinned to her cardigan. However did my grandparents cope with those farewells? (I'm thankful that they did: it was my father's evacuation to the Cotswolds and his consequent love affair with the area that made me realise at a very young age that I wanted to live here too.)

I thought I'd guessed the destination for Laura's "Ruthless Romans" topic trip. Surely it had to be either Cirencester, Chedworth Roman Villa or the Roman Baths at Bath? But no, they headed off to foreign parts – across the border into Wales for a fabulous day at Caerleon Roman Remains. The photos of the children dressed as legionnaires made it look as though they'd travelled back in time. It was a trip they will remember for the rest of their lives.

Where, then, would they go for this term's topic? It's "The Awesome Outdoors", and not, as one child first reported, "Automatic Doors". (Her mother thought this unusual theme would lead to some interesting science and technology lessons. It was several days before she realised her daughter's mistake.)

I love the alliterative titles teachers give to their topics. It's great psychology for generating excitement, but I wondered where would their "awesome" destination be? I thought about my own travels when I was Laura's age. I was lucky enough to spend my ninth year in the USA, where my father was working. We saw Yellowstone Park's geysers, the Badlands, the Grand Canyon, the Great Lakes – all pretty awesome to a child who till then had thought Sidcup was the centre of the world.

Laura produced the note from her bookbag with a flourish.

"We're going to Westonbirt Arboretum!" she cried excitedly. A pause. "Where's that again?"

Of course! Where else? The environment on our doorstep is hard to beat in terms of awesomeness. The Arboretum's education department is second to none, so I know her class will have a fabulous, memorable time and come back filled with wonder.

To children, any trip is far from school if it requires a coach to get them there – and there should just about be time for a sing-song on the way. There'll be plenty of opportunities for globe-trotting when she grows up.

Home from Home

May 2012

Living as I do in an area that's a tourist destination, I'm always curious when I go away on holiday to see whether I can find tourist spots that are equally homely. It's rare to find another place that's a match for our little corner of the Cotswolds.

I'm therefore taken aback to come across a small Scottish town that seems on first glance to meet my demanding criteria.

Late one afternoon, en route in our camper van from Perth to the coast of Fife, we encounter a small market town with a familiar air. Spotting brown tourist information signs to a nearby castle, we decide to stay the night and visit it in the morning. We find a place to park near the centre of town, and while my husband reads the paper and my daughter plays with her toys, I combine a recce with a run (I'm in training for the Bristol 10K).

I gently jog down the narrow high street, making a mental note of the facilities. There's a craft bakers, an award-winning butchers, two charity shops with a high class of junk, and a useful old-fashioned hardware shop. There are signs to a library and a leisure centre and an edge-of-town supermarket. (Sound familiar, anyone?)

The calorific perils of a chippy, a Chinese and an Indian takeaway are offset by a slimming club in the old market hall, which also hosts a café offering hearty soups, sandwiches and cakes. (Well, this is Scotland).

I jog on to the end of town and I'm immediately amidst farmland, where fingerposts beckon me on to pleasant footpaths through sheep-strewn green fields.

Hmmm, this is home from home, I think. I could get to like this place. There's even a local royal connection, albeit not one ever to make the pages of *Hello* magazine: Mary, Queen of Scots, was once a guest, and later a prisoner, at the local castle.

Turning left onto a footpath, I jog happily round the perimeter of the town and am rewarded with a glimpse of the castle, in the middle of a small loch. I pause to catch my breath by the ticket office and mentally book a family boat trip to it for tomorrow. Culture, a boat and a spooky-looking setting that would do Scooby-Doo proud – there's something here to keep all the family happy.

When I head back into town, the charity shops are opposite me, and I notice for the first time that they are in aid of a Scottish children's hospice. A little further down the road, in the direction of the other end of town, is a sign to that very hospice. A few yards on I pass the high school. It is closed down and boarded up, peppered with danger signs. I'm sure there's no connection between the closure of the (dangerous) school and the presence of a children's hospice, but it still makes me shudder with horror. I'm so sad for the children affected by either building.

I run on, hoping to find something cheery to negate the effect of these discoveries. Ahead of me is a large building, by far the most grand and imposing on the high street. I run a little faster, spirits rising. Level with the gated entrance, I read the sign.

It is a funeral directors.

Now feeling thoroughly chilled, I turn on the heel of my trainers and plod back to the van, to find my family waiting. I couldn't live here, not amidst all this sadness. After all, there is no place like home.

From Diamond to Silver: Remembering the 25th Anniversary of the Queen's Coronation

June 2012

What will you remember about the Queen's Diamond Jubilee? In a town like Tetbury, so conscious of its royal connections, there will certainly be plenty of celebrations to choose from. But in twenty years' time, what will be your most vivid memories of the occasion?

If my experience is anything to go by, they may surprise you.

My daughter recently announced what for her had been the best thing about William and Kate's wedding a year ago. (To you and me, the passage of a year is nothing, but when you're eight, that's a big proportion of your life – certainly long enough to make you nostalgic.)

At the time, she celebrated the event in all the ways I thought she should: watched the wedding ceremony live on telly, joined in our local street party, had a non-uniform day at school, went to a party at Brownies. But her fondest memory was none of these things.

"I was thinking of writing a letter to Prince William and Kate," she revealed, "to thank them for making it such a special day for me."

I raised my eyebrows. "And what are you going to say?"

"Well, I was going to thank them for getting married because if they hadn't, there wouldn't have been a street party, and it was at the street party that I started to become really good friends with Nicola, and we hadn't known each other very well before then."

And there was I fondly hoping that my invention of a Hunt the Corgi game might have been the highlight.

I shouldn't have been so surprised. My own recollections of national celebrations when I was young are equally unexpected. I was a teenager during the Queen's Silver Jubilee. Though living abroad, I was spending the summer in England staying with my grandmother, and I had my teenage Dutch boyfriend in tow. I remember my grandfather giving us each a Silver Jubilee coin, and there being a lot of silvery stuff and British flags in the shops, but my most vivid memory is of the rivalry with my boyfriend over whose country had the better Queen. To my mind, there could only be one right answer, but my faith in Britain's supremacy was a little shaken when he told me proudly that his forebears had once sailed up the Thames in anger and taken possession of the Isle of Sheppey, something the history lessons at my school in England had singularly failed to mention. By the time the Wimbledon finals came round, our rivalry was intense.

It astonishes me now to have to relate that in 1977, both our nations were represented in the Ladies' Singles Final: Virginia Wade playing for England and Betty Stove for the Netherlands. To get that far, they had put out in earlier rounds – wait for it – tennis legends Martina Navratilova, Chris Evert and Billie Jean King. It was as if this year's tournament had been fixed specifically to emphasise the differences between me and my boyfriend.

So my strongest memory of the Silver Jubilee is of sitting on the swirly carpet of my grandmother's living room, tense and shouting alongside my equally vociferous boyfriend, as we watched our nations do battle on the tennis court. I was convinced that Wade would win, as if by some kind of divine right – which was only as it should be in our Queen's special year of celebrations. And win she did, but only after dropping the first set, to the detriment of my fingernails. Watching her hold her silver plate above her head was a truly historic moment. Gracious and elated in my victory, I didn't realise the Dutch boyfriend would soon be history too.

However you choose to spend the Jubilee weekend, may it bring you many happy memories.

The Olympic Spirit Meets Britannia

July/August 2012

With the opening ceremony of London 2012 nearly upon us, I have to say that I'm entirely happy with my experience of the Games to date: watching the Olympic Torch pass by.

I didn't want to miss the opportunity for my daughter Laura to see a piece of history in the making. About to turn nine the next day, she would remember the event for the rest of her life. It would also be the perfect overture to her birthday party, the theme of which was to be the Olympic Games (albeit our games largely featuring the garden hosepipe, making the most of the fleeting heatwave).The timing couldn't have been better.

And so after school on the Tuesday afternoon, we shot off down the A46 to park near my brother's and sister's houses, a stone's throw from the Bath to Bristol road. I'd have preferred to see the Torch crossing the Clifton Suspension Bridge, enabling us to segue neatly from Laura's current school topic (Brunel) to the next one (The Olympic Games), but it would have meant missing a morning of school.

We strolled down to the Torch route at 5 o'clock and the sun was scorching. We quickly claimed a piece of (hot) pavement from which we could enjoy an unimpeded view and sat down to see what would happen next.

We weren't really sure what to expect, but somehow I thought there'd be something to imbue us with the Olympic spirit, inspiring us to strive "faster, higher, stronger". I thought there would be an international vibe to the proceedings, in preparation for so many nations coming together.

I thought to myself, if this was America, there'd be marching bands with drum majorettes and baton twirlers, military precision and grandeur and pomp and show. If it was China, there'd be military might and vast crowds of synchronised dancers in colourful costumes.

But this was Britain, and what unfolded was an endearingly British spectacle. Here was the general public at its whimsical British best, turning pink in the hot sun without sunhats or sunblock, tucking into Mr Whippy's 99s and making their own entertainment.

Several small children had brought along their own Olympic Torches, home-made in the best Blue Peter tradition, all sticky-backed plastic and kitchen tinfoil. Many waved Union flags, dusted off from last year's Royal

Wedding and being given a preliminary airing in preparation for the Royal Jubilee. With a wry flourish, my brother produced a free promotional flag that he'd been given by a building company at the height of last year's Will-and-Kate mania. The building company had since gone bust.

Amiable security guards, armed only with DayGlo yellow waistcoats and walkie talkies, ambled about the crowds, trying to look busy to justify their temp agency fee. They were clearly at a bit of a loose end. One of them, with spectacular dreadlocks, suddenly seized a home-made Olympic Torch from a child and started to run along the route, waving at the spectators as if he were the official Torch bearer. A Mexican wave of cheers followed him. Then a couple of cyclists, having jumped the road blocks, pedalled cheerfully along the centre of the cleared street to further applause.

Finally it was time for the real thing, heralded by pairs of police cars driving slowly and officiously along. But their windows were wound right down and the policemen inside were relaxed and smiling, proffering royal waves. Then came the sponsors' open-topped buses, understaffed, a few souls in garish uniforms looking slightly embarrassed as they waved to the crowds. But the crowds didn't care: they just let out a rousing cheer.

At last along came the Olympic bus (but it didn't appear to be faster, stronger or higher). Jogging behind, holding the Torch aloft, was an elderly white-bearded sage. He looked as if he'd just come down from Mount Olympus, waving and saluting as he trotted along, clearly savouring every moment of his 300 metres of fame. The crowd went wild.

And then he'd passed by and it was over. We all dispersed quickly and quietly, ripples of innocent pleasure radiating out through suburban streets. There wasn't a hint of trouble. We'd all got more than we bargained for: a bit of a laugh, unscheduled sunshine, a Mr Whippy and some community bonding.

I came home very glad to be British.

Putting the Great Back into Britain

September 2012

Back in the spring, with the calendar dominated by the Queen's Diamond Jubilee and the London 2012 Olympics, I expected our lives would feel a little empty come September. What on earth could we look forward to after all that summer treasure: diamonds, gold, silver and bronze?

Yet with the Autumn Term upon us, I'm still remarkably buoyed up by all the excitement. The Olympics have left us a wealth of unexpected legacies, quite apart from the planned regeneration of East London. Here are some of the things that the Young household has gained, my nine-year-old daughter Laura's points first:

1) A greater awareness of the world beyond the Cotswolds, its many countries, nationalities and ethnic diversity.

2) An encyclopaedic knowledge of these countries' national flags.

3) A keen interest in – and mostly, but not always, the ability to spell – numerous sports that she'd never heard of before this summer.

4) An awareness of history being made all around her – she'll have plenty of memories to share with her grandchildren, beginning every story with "I was there when..."

This is what I have gained from the London 2012 Olympics:

5) The totally new experience of wanting to read a newspaper backwards rather than forwards. Previously the most use I've had for the sports section has been to line the cat litter tray.

6) A huge sense of relief that our beautiful national flag has been reclaimed from dodgy punk rockers and right wing fanatics, to be flourished now with unremitting pride.

7) A renewed respect for the Royal Family. If that fabulous double act by the Queen and James Bond doesn't soften the hearts of the hardest Republicans, then nothing ever will.

8) A passionate longing to have one of those long-legged swimsuits that triathletes wear – and the figure to go with it. Watch my personal space – I'll be taking up less of it from now on.

9) A genuine conviction that the main role of British athletes at international sporting events is not to provide comic relief, but to win medals and inspire generations to come with their talent, dedication and single-mindedness.

Even my husband, a proud Scottish republican, gained from this summer's outpouring of British pride: so that Laura and I could enjoy the festivities unrestrained, we gave him free rein to go off and climb Scottish mountains all summer (Munro-bagging, as it's known north of the border).

I know I've always been a bit of a Pollyanna, ever able to irritate gloomy friends with my 'when life gives you lemons, make lemonade' attitude. But now I'm sure there's a much broader optimism afoot – a national conviction, in fact. We may no longer rule the waves, but boy, do we know how to make them. It's been a truly Great British summer. I've forgotten and forgiven the rain.

In Praise of Pine Cones – and Grandpa

October 2012

On my way to a routine hospital appointment, I'm strolling down a suburban street when I spot a perfect pine cone lying on a grass verge. Now, I cannot pass a nice pine cone any more easily than I can ignore a conker, freshly dispensed in all its shiny glory from the spiky lime-green case in which it's been lying, fattening, since Spring. I slip the pine cone into my pocket, glad to be distracted from my imminent arthritis check-up. I've been a bit creaky lately and I'm not looking forward to my consultant's review.

Pine cones, in contrast, are full of the promise of good things: cosy autumn firesides; sustenance for small birds in winter; nourishment for squirrels as they bulk up for hibernation. Pine cones are a forerunner of Christmas, but in a more subtle way than the charity gift catalogues that have been landing on my doormat since July.

I always plan to collect and decorate pine cones and string them on the Christmas tree with tartan ribbon. If my daughter gets her way, they'll be adorned with fake snow and glitter too. Or else we'll douse them in melted fat, roll them in seeds and crumbs, and suspend them with string from trees outside our living room window. They provide an oasis for hungry birds on short, dark winter days, and it's a pleasure to watch from inside a warm house.

There's an unnatural neatness about the shape of a pine cone. They're reminiscent of the children's drawings of Christmas trees that subdue nature's disorder into a more manageable form. But even so, a pine cone is a pine cone is a pine cone.

Or so I thought until last weekend, when, on a walk in a Penzance park with my father, I learned to appreciate the pine cone in a different way. Just turned 80, he is a long-time lover of trees and their diversity. Stooping to collect a pine cone from the ground, he gave my nine-year-old daughter a spontaneous lesson in the identification of the originating tree, based on the arrangement and distribution of its spikes.

Unlike me, my father has an artist's eye, full of wonder at the natural architecture of the world about us. An accomplished watercolourist, woodturner, carpenter and calligrapher, he has a keen understanding of the complexity of the tree's task in creating what it has so casually dropped in our path. No matter what your religious beliefs, when you've heard my father hold forth about trees, you can't help but be in awe of nature, and his childlike sense of wonder is not restricted to trees. He's ready to detect a miracle in everything he sees in the natural world.

I believe this attitude is one of many reasons why, at the age of 80, he remains so youthful in spirit and outlook – and why my small daughter relates so readily to his world view. She is as close to him as his shadow. They spend many happy hours together. Lately he's taught her to paint in watercolours. We have a pair of paintings, one by him, the other by her, hanging in our living room, natural companion pieces. This summer, both of them took first prize in their respective age groups in the "original painting" category of our local village show. I see echoed in their relationship the closeness of my connection with my own Grandma, my father's mother. It seems the baton of the bond is being handed down the generations.

So, with my pine cone resting snugly in my pocket, I settle down in the hospital waiting room, beginning to feel a little more optimistic about my appointment. I know I can depend upon my lovely consultant to be supportive, and I'm sure she'll have some sound advice for keeping me young by nature, as well as young by name. I want to make sure that when my turn comes to connect with my grandchildren, I'll be ready to rise to the challenge. Goodness knows, I've got a hard act to follow.

Books on the Brain

November 2012

When the first charity Christmas catalogue dropped through my letterbox, I was not best pleased. After all, I was in the middle of packing to go on my summer holiday.

I was irritated also by spotting the first mince pies in the supermarket in September. In fact, I generally try to avoid any mention of Christmas until after Guy Fawkes Night is over and done with.

But last year, I left my preparations until a little too close to Christmas, and, to my shame, completely failed to send cards to half my friends and relations. Nearly a year later, I'm still cringing with guilt that I didn't send one to my best friend's elderly mother, who, in her late 80s and unwell, still managed to send one to me. I'm determined to be better organised this year. Gladys, this month's column's for you.

Late October, my sister-in-law makes a helpful pre-emptive strike, initiating a discussion about what we should buy each other for Christmas. She suggests that it would be easier if we stopped buying for the adults in the family at all, focusing only on the children. *Great*, I think, *I'm off the hook!* But her proposal is scuppered by immediate protests from my brother and sister, both older than me but big kids at heart. So I resign myself to writing my Christmas shopping list – or at least the list of names of whom I have to buy for.

I have little time or enthusiasm for shopping. I barely enter a grocery store from one month to the next. (Whoever invented Ocado home deliveries, I salute you.) I therefore hit on a new tactic to minimise the pain and effort: this year, I resolve to buy everything in just one shop. I need to send so many presents by post that this one shop must sell goods that are easy to wrap and fit in a Jiffy bag – so that's the hardware shop off the list, then.

I try empathising with the recipients. What would I ask Santa for myself? (Oh, if only he'd consult me!) I jot down some ideas. They are all books. I'm constantly hearing snippets of intriguing books on BBC Radio 4, to which I'm addicted. Whenever I follow through and buy them, I'm never disappointed. In fact, I often enjoy them so much that I pass them on to friends or buy second copies to hand out. So this year I shall buy everyone books. Easy to wrap, easy to post – what's not to love about a book?

Some of my most treasured possessions are books, such as the small red hardbacks of *Alice's Adventures in*

Wonderland and *Through The Looking Glass*, previously owned by my mother when she was a child. Both our names are inscribed on the fly leaf, mine in red crayon in the shaky infant school hand that preceded learning to do joined-up writing.

My single most precious thing is a small brown statuette of a man reading a book. He sat on my grandmother's mantelpiece throughout my childhood and he moved in with me when she died. If I choose carefully, I could be giving my friends not only a Christmas present but a lifelong treasure.

There must surely be a book to suit the tastes of everyone on anyone's Christmas list. A few ideas already spring to mind for the adults, but with children, I worry about duplication. But they can always pass swaps on to friends as birthday presents, or re-gift them, as now seems to be the accepted euphemism for getting rid of presents you hate. Signed copies provide a thoughtful point of difference. I've been lucky enough to snap up a book signed by both Julia Donaldson and Axel Scheffler at Bath Literature Festival for one child on my list (*Gruffalo* fans will be envious), but what should I get the others?

For inspiration, I turn to my daughter, aged nine. An avid reader, she currently enjoys any book featuring kittens, puppies, or mermaids –preferably all three.

"What do you think is the best book you've ever read?" I ask her.

She thinks hard for a moment, then gives a big smile, tricky problem resolved.

"I haven't read it yet," she asserts with confidence.

While I applaud her optimism, I am no further forward. Time to consult the local bookshop, whose staff will know what's new and what's hot. And if I look sharp, I can just fit them in on my way to the Post Office to buy my Christmas stamps.

And in case I forget in next month's column: Happy Christmas, everyone!

Meeting Our (Rugby) Match Provides a Family Outing

December 2012/January 2013

Recently I did something I've never done before: I watched my first live rugby match. Actually, forget the live – it was my first rugby match of any kind.

A city centre stadium would not normally lure me away from our cottage fireside on a chilly Sunday afternoon, but I was subject to a force of nature: Hurricane Laura, aka my nine-year-old daughter.

Laura had been taking part in a tag rugby course at school, run by an outreach coach from Bristol Rugby Club. Always keen to try a new sport, Laura threw herself into the game in a style all of her own. Rather than jostling competitively with the other children, she trotted round picking up the tags as they were dropped, politely handing them back to the players who'd lost them. She does like things to be tidy.

At the end of the course, the Rugby Club kindly gave a free match ticket to every child who had taken part. Ah, those outreach folk are smart: how many junior school children are likely to go to a rugby match unaccompanied? Consequently every child's family had to buy at least one adult ticket. As the match fell on a Sunday afternoon, when most families like to do something together, most of the rugby-playing children had more than one parent in tow. One little girl even took her grandparents and baby brother too.

And so it was that on Sunday afternoon, with woolly hats, thermos flask and gritted teeth, we dutifully took our place in the stands. (Stands? What's that about? Why not seats? I thought rugby was meant to be a civilised game.) Our spirits lifted a little when we spotted the stadium's cafe selling piping hot pasties. Well, rugby does burn off a lot of calories. But to my surprise, I soon found myself distracted from my pasty by the game. This I did not expect.

As the match got underway, I discovered that it was like watching ballet without music in which all the dancers are on 6,000 calories a day. Although the players had legs like tree trunks and the physical resilience of a tank, they had real balletic grace. As they surged across the pitch, entirely focused on seizing the ball, their raw power reminded me of lions hunting gazelles on an African plain. Actually, it was more like lions hunting lions. I especially liked it when, for some reason I did not understand, a smaller player was pitched up above the scrum, half leaping, half hurled into the air. The only damper on my enjoyment was worrying about whether they'd hurt themselves.

By half time, my grasp of the rules was still slim. It was a breakthrough moment when I realised that the total on the right of the scoreboard was not the second team's score but the number of minutes that had been played. No wonder the team I'd thought was losing was looking so cheerful.

As the game drew to a close, I looked down at my daughter. She had spent the first half playing on the steps with her friends, before sharing a portion of chips with them at the interval. For the whole of the second half, she had been completely engrossed in a sticker book, neatly dressing up dolls in foreign costumes. The closest she'd come to watching the match was getting the autograph of a man in a bear costume serving as the home team's mascot.

But never mind, I think she got her money's worth for her ticket.

Tales of the Unexpected Book

February 2013

Beware of the *Tetbury Advertiser* – you never know where it might lead! I mean that in the nicest possible way, for a few years ago, the *Advertiser* was the starting point of a trail that led to the publication of my first book. Here's the tale of how it came about.

In the summer of 2010, a few months after I'd started writing my Young By Name column in the *Tetbury Advertiser*, I was contacted by one of its regular readers, the writer Paul Newnton. Though now living on the other side of the country, he kept up with local news via a postal subscription to this popular monthly magazine. Having enjoyed my column, Paul asked me to help him promote his new novel, the first in a proposed series. Despite my protest that I had no experience of book promotion, I agreed to meet him for tea in the Snooty Fox on his next trip to Tetbury. With the help of an excellent cream tea, he convinced me that by drawing on my long career in journalism, PR and marketing, I could be of valuable assistance. He was right: within a very short time, I'd arranged for his book to be stocked in the Yellow-Lighted Bookshop, generated news coverage in the local press, and fixed up an interview on BBC Radio Gloucestershire.

A few weeks later, a graphic designer friend mentioned that his wife, who runs the Bristol-based assisted publishing company, SilverWood Books, was enjoying the online version of my Young By Name blog. We arranged to meet, and I came away with a commission to write a self-help promotion handbook for authors. The book was particularly to address the rapidly expanding group of self-published or independent authors – but what author doesn't want to sell more books, even those commissioned by traditional publishers?

To explain the jargon, self-published authors are those who produce their books independently of traditional publishing companies. Thanks to the latest developments in digital printing and e-book technology, it's possible to put your book on the market without a publisher's contract, thus avoiding the nerve-wracking round of submissions and rejection letters. Authors who are willing and able to master the necessary technology do this themselves, but for technophobes – or for those who prefer to spend their time writing – there exist excellent publishing consultants who can do this for them, adding value and expertise. These are far removed from the "vanity publishers" of the past, who simply took your money and treated your manuscript as a routine print job, often with dire results.

To fulfil my commission, I undertook extensive research, interviewing many authors – including Tetbury's Paul Newnton, of course – and members of the book trade, not least Hereward Corbett, proprietor of Tetbury's Yellow-Lighted Bookshop.

Pre-publication, the first reviewer of *Sell Your Books!* was so enthusiastic that she even agreed to write a foreword. This was no small compliment, as this reviewer was Dr Alison Baverstock, senior lecturer in the MA in Publishing at Kingston University and all-round publishing guru. She deems it to give "motivating, practical and cheerful guidance on the process. It raises the spirits and promotes author confidence. It's an investment in your writing now – and your future development".

In another bizarre demonstration of all roads leading to Tetbury, I discovered that I'd met Alison a few years before, when I was working at Westonbirt School and she was guest speaker at Speech Day. I'd taken her photo to include in the school's newsletter.

I hope that, knowing its local origins and inspiration, authors living in and around Tetbury will take a special interest in my book. I'd love to hear any feedback or input from them, which I might also be able to share, with their permission, on my blog of book promotion tips for authors at Off the Shelf Book Promotions.

Finally, a big thank you to the wonderful Barry Gibbs, editor of the marvellous multi-faceted *Tetbury Advertiser*, for commissioning my Young By Name column in the first place. Without you, none of this might have happened!

On a Mission to Post a Parcel

March 2013

Ash Wednesday finds me on the high street of a town that's new to me, searching for a Post Office in which I can post an important parcel.

I'm up against the clock, because I've left my husband and daughter parked in a restricted zone where the parking ticket for our camper van, in which we've come away for half term, is about to run out. I march purposefully through the pedestrian precinct, scanning the shop fronts on either side of me for the familiar red oval logo.

After a few minutes of fruitless searching, I've passed endless charity shops and Poundstores, two pawnbrokers, a halal butcher and a surprising number of greengrocers displaying neat, open baskets of exotic fruit and vegetables, the kind that characterise Asian and Caribbean cookery. I've given a wide berth to 'Jackpots', a tacky arcade of slot machines offering prizes of up to £500, according to big signs in the window. Just 90 minutes' drive from Tetbury, we might as well be in a different country. No cosy tearooms, antique shops or bookstores are to be seen. There'll be no rich pickings in this high street's charity shops.

With a glance at my watch, I give up trying to find the Post Office on my own. I am not my husband: I will ask someone for directions. But spotting a helpful-looking person is not easy. Everyone I encounter is pale, downcast, jaded and sad. Their clothes are cheap, dark and drab, with one exception – a podgy fellow in his twenties sports a black hoodie to the front of which are stitched brightly-coloured, giant metallic dollar signs. From the rest of his ensemble, I infer that these indicate his aspirations rather than his bank balance.

If I accost any of these passers-by, they look as if they might burst into tears.

Then at last, like buses, two friendly faces crop up at once. There on a street corner are two smartly dressed young men, standing quietly, looking about them as if at a loose end. They are quick to make eye contact with me and flash me a smile. Emboldened, I approach them.

"Excuse me, can you please point me in the direction of the nearest Post Office?" I plead.

Their smiles broaden.

"No problem," says one, "it's right there."

He points to the other side of the street. The Post Office, based within a shabby convenience store, is exactly opposite where I am standing. I've been too preoccupied with people-watching to spot it. About to mumble an embarrassed apology for my stupidity, I cast my eyes downward. They alight on the young men's lapels, where I spot badges identifying them as members of a church known for sending young missionaries out into foreign parts. I do not envy them their task in this dismal town. It's my turn to flash a smile.

"Thank you so much!" I beam. "You've been very helpful."

I think they will need all the encouragement they can get if they are to make it through their duties today. If I can't summon up the resolve to ask the locals for directions, how hard must it be to talk to them about saving their souls?

But as I join the queue in the Post Office, I castigate myself for my arrogance. Though armed only with smart suits and old-fashioned haircuts, these pleasant young men are bolstered by a much greater force than my smile: their unshakeable belief in their god. Though I don't share their faith, I hugely admire what they are doing. I am suddenly moved to pay tribute, and so, my own mission accomplished, as I march back to the car where my husband will be impatiently drumming the steering wheel, I determine to show some resolution of my own. I decide to give up alcohol for Lent.

Mysterious ways...

Living with a Fussy Eater

April 2013

"Mummy, can I please have some really yummy bacon for breakfast today?"

"Bacon? Are you sure?"

The smell of sizzling bacon demolishes the resolve of many a vegetarian. It seems my nine-year-old daughter Laura is not immune.

"Yes, because I haven't had bacon for such a long time."

She sounds accusing, but she has only herself to blame. She turned vegetarian two Christmases ago. This surprised me at the time, because her favourite food was bacon, and not just any old bacon – She was especially fond of the ready-cooked crispy kind, eaten cold. My nephew called it "sun-dried pig". Ever since then, she has eschewed (but not chewed) all kinds of meat, other than the occasional sausage (so not much meat at all, then). Her favourite form of sausage is the battered kind from chip shops. I suppose that'll be her Scottish genes coming through.

"I don't think I could eat bacon from a pig I knew personally," she declares a little later, tucking into a couple of rashers.

Round here, that's not such an unlikely occurrence – she often exchanges pleasantries with creatures destined for the shelves of local shops. We buy meat from a lovely organic farm which was until recently home to a pair of pigs called "Bacon" and "More Bacon".

But this time Laura's craving proves to be a flash in the pan. Next day, she's back on the vegetable wagon. I'm disappointed. As she's not fond of cheese, egg yolks or nuts, providing her with sufficient protein without the use of meat is a challenge.

That's not the problem with my husband. He's an enthusiastic carnivore. When he says, "I could eat a horse", he actually means it. With him, it's the carbs that are the catch. He is extraordinarily particular.

"I don't really like rice, you know," he announces one day after demolishing a delicious Indian meal.

"I'm not that fond of pasta." This, after an excellent seafood pasta bake.

"Why does anyone bother with white bread?" What's not to love about Hobbs's finest?

Finding a meal that will please both him and my daughter has never been easy. To throw another complication into the blender, they both have Type 1 diabetes. This means every meal has to be low fat and low GI (i.e. its carbohydrate content should release very slowly, to keep blood sugars even).

To provide a suitable meal without losing my sanity, I try to remain philosophical, following my grandmother's advice: "Moderation in all things, including moderation."

Another source of comfort in the kitchen is the remembered wisdom of my lovely late friend Eileen. Once on the staff of The Snooty Fox in Tetbury, she went on to run a prestigious gentleman's club in London. It was no wonder as she had a wonderful way with food and drink, including the ability to truly enjoy it. Even when chemotherapy was playing havoc with her own taste buds, she was a wonderful host and cook. The last time I went to her house for lunch, she presented a meal fit for a king: beautifully arranged slices of Parma ham and melon on exquisite plates. Come to think of it, she may actually have catered for kings in the past, or at least for minor members of the nobility.

I also appreciated Eileen's refreshingly creative approach to dieting.

“There aren’t any calories in anything you eat standing up,” she would assert. “Nor in anything you eat from someone else’s plate.”

So this Easter, whatever I have to cook to keep the rest of the family happy, I’m going to have a little of what I fancy. I just need to remember to put the Easter eggs on my husband’s plate and to eat them standing up. There, no harm done.

Happy Easter, everyone!

There's No Place Like Home

May 2013

What a difference a holiday makes! And not only because it brings you new experiences. I also love the fresh perspective that a holiday gives me on my home.

To give my house the best chance of pleasing me when I return, I always tidy it to the point of exhaustion before we go away. This Easter, the night before we leave for Luxembourg, I am still whizzing around the house at 2am. Dorothy the cat is the only one awake to witness my late-night vigil. Together we excavate unknown territory (the bottom of the ironing basket), empty the dishwasher and clear our vast kitchen table. Finally, we banish the clutter from the foot of the stairs, as no-one else has taken the hint to take it upstairs and put it away. After just five hours' sleep, I rise again to pack.

Holidaying in a camper van demands a completely different packing technique from other forms of travel. You cut out the middleman that is the suitcase, instead stashing everything directly into cupboards and cubbyholes dotted around the van. Everything not actively in use is out of sight. This enforced minimalism is refreshing and liberating when you're used to the clutter that comes of living in the same house for twenty years.

Camper van holidays are also necessarily communal, requiring the family to share a single room for the duration. There's no retreating to separate studies and computers. Instead we assemble each evening around the small single table to play endless old-technology games. We never tire of cards, especially now that our daughter is big enough to manage a hand without having to spread her cards out in full view on the table in front of her. We write things: in our daughter's case, poems and songs about toilets (I'm rather hoping this is just a phase); crossword solutions in my husband's; and travelogues if you're, er, me. We read books. I read more books in this fortnight-long trip that I've read in the preceding three months. We relax.

After two weeks on mainland Europe, with strong winds making it feel as if there are speed bumps on the English Channel, we return from Calais. As ever, I'm heartened by my first glimpse of the White Cliffs of Dover. As they loom into view, I think, as always, how comforting they must have looked to those war-time evacuees from Dunkerque. Yet I'm never as heartened as, when joining the

A46 from the motorway, I see the first signs to our more local Petty France and Dunkirk, the familiar Cotswold drystone walls flanking our route.

Unlocking the door of our cottage, I cross the threshold nervously, seeing my house as if through the eyes of a stranger. Of course, everything is just as we left it. Only I am not. And for both of these things, I am thankful.

The Woolsack by Any Other Name

June 2013

With the end of May heralding the Cotswolds' most idiosyncratic sporting events – the Tetbury Woolsack Races and the Cooper's Hill Cheese-Rolling – I've been thinking about the inextricable link between event and setting. These two ancient rites would not attract the same following if removed to other places. Hefting a Woolsack the length of Chipping Sodbury's level high street or rolling a cheese through Bourton-on-the-Water would be nowhere near as exciting.

You can stage a marathon anywhere in the world, but it will never be the same race. Ask anyone who has run in London, Paris, New York, or, er, Marathon.

This fact first dawned on me when, in my pre-baby running days, my husband and I signed up to enter the Cheltenham 10K.

This will be a sedate little number, we thought, passing elegant Georgian facades and corporation planting. We warmed up with a few shorter runs: a pleasant 5K jaunt around Bourton-on-the-Water, followed by the Chippenham River Run, both events equally defined by their setting. The post-race refreshments left a bit to be desired, but we were looking forward to Cheltenham's more genteel offering: cucumber sandwiches and Earl Grey, perhaps?

But it was not to be. A week before the race, a letter announced that due to unforeseen circumstances (a row between the Town Council and the event organisers), the race would now take place at the Moreton-in-Marsh Fire Service College. *OK*, we thought, *Moreton-in-Marsh is pretty too. Not a problem.*

Only on arrival did we discover that the College is set well away from the town and offers quite a different scenario: surreal mock-ups of emergencies in which firefighters may hone their skills. We ran past crashed aeroplanes, burnt-out buildings, overturned railway carriages and motorway pile-ups. It was like fleeing from the apocalypse. Well, that's one way to cut minutes off your personal best.

Which is why I'm particularly pleased to be organising a race this month in a much more peaceful setting: what's dubbed by local runners "The Yellow Brick Road" – the level stretch of the Cotswold Way that skirts Hawkesbury

Upton, with fine views down to the Severn Valley. On a clear day, both Severn Bridges wink back at you in the sunshine. The HU5K Run will take place on Saturday 15 June, starting at 10am, giving woolsack-toting cheese-rolling racers a couple of weeks to get their puff back first. All ages (seven+) and abilities are welcome. Leading the way will be former Team GB Olympic runner Nick Rose, veteran of the Olympics in Moscow in 1980 and Los Angeles in 1984. Now there's a man who can tell you what a difference a venue makes.

Where Do Cats Go for Their Summer Holidays?

July/August 2013

Like most parents of school-age children, I'm counting down the days till the end of term. I can't wait to ditch the school-run/clubs/homework routine in favour of the anarchy that is the school summer holiday. But planning for the holidays this summer will be more complicated, because we now have a cat.

Dorothy Purrkins, as my daughter christened her, moved in on the snowiest day in January. An adaptable, sociable animal, she'd go with the flow, whatever our chaotic household threw at her. So quickly did she adjust to our routines that I wondered whether she'd previously had us under surveillance.

When other cats entered "her" garden, she'd chase them off her territory with gusto. When we had human visitors, she'd greet them on equal terms, confident that they would be pleased to see her (which they always were).

After six months in residence, she's calling the shots. When her food bowl is empty, she sits next to it, politely but firmly pinning me with a laser-like look until we replenish it. After an outing to the garden, she stands on the window-ledge, staring with the intensity only a cat can muster until we open the window to let her in. Seated companionably in the sitting room of an evening, her eyes follow us proprietorially around the room. We should have called her Mona Lisa.

But what will happen when we go away to Scotland in the summer? I worry that, thinking we've abandoned her, she'll move on in search of a more dependable home. I could send her to a cattery for the duration, but a cat with a huge rural territory would not enjoy a fortnight penned indoors. Even with a kind friend happy to feed her while we're away, it's a tough call.

Or so I thought until this morning. After despatching husband and daughter on the school run, I was standing quietly in the utility room, enjoying a calming cup of tea before work. Dorothy Purrkins sauntered confidently past my feet, heading for the cat flap. Strolling leisurely up the garden path, she chose the best vantage point before settling down on the lawn, surveying her territory. She was a tortoiseshell Monarch of the Glen. Spoiled for choice by the many pleasurable opportunities that the garden held in store, she lay quietly considering her options. Snooze in the hammock in the shade? Warm up with a sunbathe in the greenhouse? Gaze at bits of blossom falling from the fruit trees? Chase butterflies fluttering around the gooseberry bush? Sprawl on the patio, absorbing the sun's heat stored in the stone paving slabs?

Whatever was on her agenda, Dorothy Purrkins looked utterly contented with the prospect. And so my decision was made: for her it will be a holiday at home. In fact, I might even join her. Who needs travel anyway?

The Unusual Souvenirs of Camper Van Travel

September 2013

As regular readers may know, my family's favourite mode of holiday transport is the camper van. For me, one of the many joys of camper van travel is that, no matter where you go, your vehicle gradually turns into a mobile museum of everywhere you've ever been. I don't mean we fill our van with souvenirs acquired in gift shops. I'm thinking more of everyday domestic items acquired from local shops in whichever country we're passing through.

Take the kitchenette. The kitchen roll is French, printed with puzzling slogans about champignons, whereas the tea towel depicts the Outer Hebrides. Snacks are offered up on a French tray printed with macarons. A wooden Provençal tomato punnet is now filled with wrapped Welsh sweets. Having used the last of the Belgian soups that broadened our knowledge of Flemish words for vegetables, we've just restocked the soup shelf with tartan tins of "Granny's Scotch Broth" in the North West Highlands of

Scotland. Currently in the biscuit tin are handmade lavender shortbread, purchased at the Achiltibuie Piping School Café, which was quieter than expected because the Pipers were on a summer tour of France. Admittedly some of our supplies have more prosaic origins, i.e. Tesco, but at least they came from the Inverness branch.

As I like to read books about the places we're visiting, our on-board library bears price labels from distant bookstores. (If you're ever in Inverness, seek out Leakey's.) We also buy novels from shops raising money for charities that we've never heard of. Blythe Community Care was everywhere we went this summer.

This cosmopolitan mix may simply indicate a lack of advance planning – I admit that we did once set off on a month's tour of France without a map or guidebook – but for me the eclectic atmosphere is part of the fun.

Preparing to head home after this summer's adventures, I realise that one man's exotic is another man's local. As we import our latest Scottish bounty to Gloucestershire, others will be heading away with treasures acquired in Tetbury. They'll be dropping Hobbs House crumbs into the pages of the books acquired in the Yellow-Lighted Bookshop, and remembering to tell their friends about cafés named just as eccentrically as our Highland find. Can there really be a Two Toads anywhere else?

And probably, just like me, as they walk back in through their own front door, they'll be congratulating themselves that no matter how much they've enjoyed their holiday, there really is no place like home.

All Change!

October 2013

"Mummy, did you realise that this will be the last night I go to bed as a Year 5?"

Such was the plaintive cry from my daughter's bedroom on the eve of the summer holidays. Like most children, she is averse to change, but it didn't take her long to realise that change can also bring advantages. Not least the one that stems from the deal we did when she was still at infants school: I agreed that the number of pounds in her pocket money should equal her school year. She reminded me of our agreement the minute the summer holidays began, holding out her hand expectantly, "because, technically, I'm really a Year 6 now".

Unlike my daughter, I positively embrace change. When I'm restless, rearranging the furniture makes me feel so much better. Not so my husband. Notorious for being unable to find things – glasses, car keys, wallet, shoes, daughter – even he feels it's getting out of hand when he can't find the sofa.

This autumn it won't be just my furniture that's getting a different outlook. I will be too. After being in constant employment since finishing my formal education, I've decided to go it alone. Well, I couldn't wish for a more understanding boss.

By the time this edition of the *Tetbury Advertiser* rolls off the press, I'll be working from home. I'll be writing, blogging, editing, helping other authors, and reading, reading, reading. (I like to think of reading as a job creation scheme for other authors.)

As a writer, I could – and often do – work anywhere I happen to be. But by choice I'll be working mostly at the desk in my study, overlooking my back garden, which from this viewpoint is dominated by a huge old apple tree.

The apple tree serves as a kind of arboreal calendar. Imperceptible daily changes transform it from bare branches to blossom to harvest. No matter what I'm writing, wherever my imagination has taken me, a glance out of the window provides me with a grounding reality check on where I am and what season we're in. A few weeks ago, the old tree was so full of apples that it showed more red than green. Now with only the odd scarlet dot breaking up the expanse of leaves, it just looks like it's recovering from measles. Before long I'll be able to see straight through barren branches.

Even that anticipated change doesn't make me feel downhearted. Thirteen years of driving to work at Westonbirt has cured me of autumn melancholy. Nothing puts a more positive spin on seasonal change than the National Arboretum. Even when the autumn blaze of colour disappears, the trees spring magically back to life, their skeletons revitalised by the magical fairy lights of the Enchanted Wood's Illuminated Trail. Such optimism is enough to make you look forward to midwinter.

But first, I need to rearrange my study...

Plus Ça Change...

November 2013

Last month, I announced a major change. I planned to abandon my day job at Read for Good, the Nailsworth-based national charity, to devote my time to writing.

"I can't believe you're leaving Read for Good!" said some of my friends, knowing what great work it does, encouraging children to read for pleasure (Readathon) and making life better for children in hospital by providing them with free books and storytellers (Readwell).

"I can't believe you're giving up a part-time term-time job – every working mother's dream!" said others.

It hadn't been an easy decision. We'd always planned I'd give up the day job once my husband started getting his Civil Service pension, which happened in March. We'd reckoned without the objections of my 10-year-old daughter:

"But it's *cool* having a mummy who works for Read for Good!"

No-one was surprised when, in the run-up to my last day at the office, I hedged my bets by cheekily appointing myself a Read for Good ambassador.

That's how it came about that during my first full week of supposedly writing full-time, I enjoyed not one but two excursions on behalf of the charity.

On Wednesday 9 October, I was invited to join two other local writers, Katie Fforde and Simon Sheridan, on BBC Radio Gloucestershire's excellent Chris Baxter Show. The DJ engaged us in a wide-ranging discussion of children's literacy and publishing trends, giving me the chance to explain the work of both Readathon and ReadWell to a county-wide audience.

The live broadcast took place not at the BBC's studio, but in a temporary setting to which they'd decamped for the Cheltenham Literature Festival. It was hard to resist phoning someone on my mobile to announce with fake nonchalance "Hello, I'm in The Writers' Room at Cheltenham Literature Festival..."

To stop myself getting ideas above my station, I lunched afterwards at McDonald's in Stroud. It seemed a good way to bring myself back down to earth.

Two days later, on Friday the 11th, I was back at the Festival, this time in the Queen's Hotel for Read for Good's fundraising reception. My role was to chat up the guests, which included award-winning children's authors and illustrators such as Nick Sharratt, Philip Reeve and Sarah McIntyre. Read for Good's new patron, the actor and author Sir Tony Robinson, inspired us all with a passionate speech about the power of books for young people. He cited his own experience of bunking off school as a teenager in order to spend more time in the library!

I did still manage to get some writing done last month, but I'm enjoying this ambassador malarkey. And that's before I've even started on the Ferrero Rocher…

By the way, I've discovered it is *impossible* to stack Ferrero Rocher into a pyramid as they do in the television advert (strapline: "Ah, Ambassador, with these Ferrero Rocher you are truly spoiling us"). I think they must have used Blu-Tack.

Using My Powers For Good

December 2013/January 2014

When I talked last month about my appearance on BBC Radio Gloucestershire at the Cheltenham Literature Festival, little did I imagine that they'd be interviewing me a month later to mark the launch of my new e-book, *Coming To Terms With Type 1 Diabetes: One Family's Story of Life After Diagnosis.*

This self-publishing project has come to fruition very quickly. Mid-October, I was wondering how to mark World Diabetes Day, an occasion when I like to raise funds and awareness for the Type 1 Diabetes research charity JDRF, because my husband and our daughter both have this incurable condition. With the big day looming on 14 November (same day as HRH Prince Charles's birthday – I wonder whether he knows), that didn't leave me much time.

Then I realised that by assembling relevant posts from my online blog and adding some new material, I could quickly turn out a little e-book to be sold on Amazon, with all the profits going to the charity.

Cue a few long days and late nights in front of my computer, some strategic tweeting to persuade BBC Radio 4 *Today* presenter Justin Webb to write a moving foreword (because he also has a child with Type 1 Diabetes), and a downright cheeky request to Bristol-based assisted publishing services company SilverWood Books to provide an appealing cover. Well, if you don't ask, you don't get. And, hey presto, my beautiful little e-book came into being. Oh, the wonder of digital technology that allows speedy, easy self-publishing!

Coming To Terms tells a coherent story of what it feels like to have your child diagnosed with a serious chronic illness requiring daily medical intervention. The book faces facts, but demonstrates that with optimism, positive thinking, and determination, it's possible to rebuild your family life and move on.

Early reviews have been enthusiastic, from families with or without the condition, and from medics too.

"A lovely, uplifting little book, full of insight, wit and practical know-how," says medical broadcaster, journalist and GP Dr Carol Cooper. "Beautifully written, a little treasure, as well as a ray of hope."

As Dr Cooper implies, the book's not all doom and gloom. It even ends with a song in praise of the man who first isolated insulin for medical use to keep Type 1 Diabetics alive. "So here's to you, Frederick Banting…" (to be sung to the tune of 'Mrs Robinson').

If you'd like to read the e-book but don't have a Kindle, download Amazon's free Kindle app for your smartphone, tablet or PC. Type "Debbie Young Coming To Terms" in Amazon's search box and it will magically appear, priced £1.99. After my last-minute rush, it won't be a one-day wonder for World Diabetes Day, but permanently available, raising funds for Diabetes research all year-round. After all, for children with Type 1 Diabetes, every day is Diabetes Day. That's one thing the digital age can't cure – yet.

In Praise of the *Tetbury Advertiser*

February 2014

To mark the fourth anniversary of this column, I'd like to use this month's slot to turn the spotlight on the *Tetbury Advertiser* and to praise all community magazines like it.

Although the *Tetbury Advertiser* is well-known locally, not everyone realises its true nature. No, I'm not about to reveal lurid scandals behind the scenes. If that's the kind of story you're after, you'll need to buy quite a different sort of paper – the type that exists to fill the pockets of shareholders by trading on people's misfortunes.

The *Tetbury Advertiser* is the polar opposite of commercial publications, carefully put together by hugely experienced volunteers for the benefit of the local community. Yes, volunteers. The Tetbury Lions registered charity produces the magazine for love, not money.

As well as providing interesting articles by local people and community groups, the *Advertiser* offers affordable advertising and editorial opportunities which help local businesses attract new customers. Especially in these tough economic times, such low-cost, high-profile coverage helps keep some small companies afloat. (I've gained useful business opportunities myself from readers of my monthly column.) Magazine production also provides significant regular business for a local print company.

And still it manages to make a profit – which the Tetbury Lions donate in its entirety to local good causes and charities. This profit does not come at the expense of readers, who receive the magazine for free. A free distribution policy ensures that the magazine is available to the entire local population, giving everyone the opportunity to feel a part of their community. No-one need miss out on being kept in touch with local events, not even pensioners on fixed incomes with no Internet access. That's quite an achievement.

Thus the *Advertiser* contributes significantly to the wellbeing of its readership in three important ways: helping local businesses remain viable, fostering community spirit and improving facilities and services. All three factors are particularly valuable in rural areas such as ours.

One might be forgiven for wondering whether in this Internet age, when so many local and national newspapers are under threat, community magazines such as the *Tetbury Advertiser* might be an endangered species. I have evidence to the contrary. A few years ago, trying to discover the most effective advertising media for a private school, I did a survey to discover the best-read newspapers and magazines in the households of current pupils' families.

I expected national daily newspapers and glossy magazines to be their favourites – The *Times* and the *Financial Times*, perhaps, plus *Country Life*, *Country Living* and *Tatler*. As it turned out, the papers of which they were least likely to miss an issue were local community magazines such as the *Tetbury Advertiser*. I'm therefore not surprised that this publication has been gaining size, strength and readership from year to year, along with more colour, more pages and better quality paper.

If I were in charge of the Queen's Birthday Honours List, the volunteers who dedicate so much time, all year round, to producing valuable community magazines such as the *Tetbury Advertiser* would not go unrewarded. And if Prince Charles, reading this column down the road at Highgrove, would like to take that as a hint and pass it on to his mum, that's absolutely fine by me.

Channelling Calm for the Dover to Dunkerque Ferry

March 2014

As I write this month's column, I'm just 22 miles away from becoming the *Tetbury Advertiser*'s foreign correspondent: I'm poised to cross the English Channel. In a Force 10 gale.

This morning, the idea of spending a week in February touring Northern France in our camper van has lost its charm. When we booked our passage in the dark days of December, far-off February seemed comfortingly spring-like. We knew we'd have to pack warm clothes to guard against the colder climate of a continental landmass, but did not foresee such storms.

My parents phoned before we were due to set off yesterday, just after the lunchtime shipping forecast. My mother did not exactly suggest we cancel our trip, but I'm sure that's what she was hoping to hear. My father, a former Royal Navy meteorologist, sounded positively excited on our behalf. The prospect of our trip brought back fond memories of his days serving on the HMS *Belfast* during the Korean War.

He offered us the benefit of his advice. "Just close your eyes and think of the sea as rocking you to sleep."

That might have worked when he was in his navy issue hammock, but unfortunately our chosen ferry service, DFDS, doesn't provide hammocks.

"Tinned peaches are the best thing to settle your stomach when you're seasick. Make sure you pack tinned peaches."

We have none in the larder, so I slip tinned pears and pineapple rings into my bag instead.

"We are allowed to postpone the trip to the Sunday when the forecast looks better," I tell him.

"Oh, the swell will continue for days after the storm," he assures me brightly. "That's how it was every time we set off towards Korea, as soon as we were away from the shelter of the land."

After boarding the ferry late afternoon, Laura demonstrates how many cuddly toys she can fit into one small 'Wanted On Voyage' bag while asking what our crossing will be like. I try to frame the prospect as a positive adventure.

"Think of it as crossing the Channel by rollercoaster," I suggest.

I know she's just reached the age where she loves rollercoasters.

"Will we go upside down?" she asks eagerly.

"I sincerely hope not!"

I'm thankful that the journey will be relatively short, until my husband recollects a memorable Channel crossing from his distant past.

"Once we had to wait outside the port for four hours because it was too rough to dock," he remembers. "We just had to ride the storm out at sea."

I try to banish images of the final scene of the movie *The Perfect Storm.*

So if my copy for this column turns up a little late, that'll be because we've been shipwrecked and I've resorted to old technology to submit it. But not to worry, I've got an empty Cotswold Spring water bottle in the van that I can use to send my message. I'm just hoping it has a homing instinct.

Postscript: our scheduled 10am departure on the Saturday morning was delayed till early evening. DFDS bumped us up to the 8am crossing instead – which left around 4pm. The reason for the delay? The ferries had been stuck out at sea for not four hours, but 10 hours, awaiting conditions sufficiently calm to let them dock. By *4pm, thankfully, all was calm. And my tinned pears and pineapple stayed in their tins. Phew.*

All Booked Up

April 2014

I'm writing this month's column entirely surrounded by books. No change there, my husband would say. But the spring always sees extra boxes of books arriving in the Young household, thanks to two special events.

The first of these took place last month: World Book Day (www.worldbookday.com) on 6 March. It's celebrated by schools in many ways, from dressing up as favourite book characters – especially fun when the staff join in – to running a Readathon sponsored read (though you can actually do either of those all year round).

This year, I set up a second-hand book sale at my daughter's school, selling donated books and well-worn school library rejects. Most sought after author? Enid Blyton! The children went home happy with their vintage finds, and the proceeds were sent to the fabulous ReadWell charity to buy books for children in hospital.

I was also one of several adults to share their favourite children's book with pupils. Mine was *The Adventures of Teddy*

Robinson by Joan G Robinson (there's nepotism for you). I too had a nominal connection with the book, as the little girl in the story was called Deborah, and Teddy Robinson looked very much like my bear.

But what I love most about World Book Day is its inclusiveness. Participating schools receive free £1 book vouchers for every pupil to buy special £1 World Book Day books. Thus even the poorest children may buy a brand new book, sometimes the only one they'll receive all year and the only encouragement they get outside of school to read for pleasure.

When I worked at the children's reading charity Read for Good (parent charity to Readathon and ReadWell), I heard heartrending stories of kids whose parents wouldn't allow books in the house or who destroyed any books they brought home. What tragedy or trauma must have triggered such anger and hatred?

That job also made me realise that many families do not appreciate the power of books to change lives. One young mum told me proudly, "We've only got three books in our house, and one of those is the Argos catalogue". I didn't dare ask what the other two were.

So whenever I find myself cursing the overflowing shelves in our house, I stop and count my child's bookish blessings: she is growing up in a house full of books, in an area well-served by wonderful public libraries and independent and second-hand bookshops. Not that my household needs more children's books, because I've salvaged a lot from my childhood. My daughter's current favourite book at bedtime? My old *Sue Day Annual*, about the same vintage as me.

But now it's the turn of adults' books to gain the spotlight: look out for World Book Night on 23 April. I'll report back on that one next month. So now I'm off to collect another box of books...

Well, you can never have too many books, or too many chocolate buttons.

[illegible] going up a house full of buckets [illegible] [illegible] bathtubs. Not the [illegible] household [illegible]

[illegible]

On the Run From Books

May 2014

I welcome the arrival of May with a sigh of relief, as it heralds the completion of a project that has preoccupied me since November: the launch of a new book, which I've co-authored with the writer and poet Dan Holloway. It's called *Opening Up To Indie Authors*, and its purpose is to build better relationships between self-published authors and the traditional book trade.

Tetbury's own book trade, in the shape of Yellow-Lighted Bookshop proprietor Hereward Corbett, gets an honorary mention in the book, the launch of which has taken me far beyond Tetbury. At the start of the school holidays, we pointed our camper van east as I'd been invited to speak at the Cambridge Literary Festival. The venue for my talk was the exotically-named Divinity Lightfoot Room in St John's College. I thought Divinity Lightfoot would make a great name for a Bond girl, so I was slightly disappointed to discover it's actually just the name of a lecture room in the College's School of Divinity.

Two days later, I was taking the stage at the London Book Fair, officially launching the book along with Dan and our editor Orna Ross, founder of the Alliance of Independent Authors. (I'm Commissioning Editor of that organisation's blog.) I admit it was a very small stage – more of a window-box, as one reporter put it – but it was exciting all the same. The huge scale of the Fair made me wonder afresh how any bookstore proprietor chooses which books to stock.

I also admire Hereward Corbett's knack for so often bringing to give talks in Tetbury authors who are on the cusp of becoming bestsellers or have just had their book chosen as BBC Radio 4's Book of the Week.

Then it was back home to collect a big box of books from the library. Just what our house needs, more books...

Fortunately for the state of my overcrowded bookshelves, these books will soon be on their way out again, destined to be thrust into the hands of random strangers.

Well, not quite random strangers – but, as part of the World Book Night initiative, I'll be giving them to adults who don't normally read books, to encourage them to enjoy reading. It's a bit like the World Book Day event for children, but for grown-ups. World Book Night kicked off in 2011, and, to my delight, I've been a designated book giver every year. Being able to give away free books, paid for by The Reading Agency, makes you feel like Father Christmas, and recipients are always grateful, especially when they realise there's no catch.

To volunteer for next year's event, visit www.worldbooknight.org.

After that, I'll be moving on to a much less bookish project: rounding up runners for the next HU5K Run. This takes place on Saturday 14 June on a mostly flat stretch of the Cotswold Way, starting and finishing at Hawkesbury Upton. If you're interested in taking part, you'll find full details on the website: www.hu5k.org. Funnily enough, I've got quite a few books about running...

WI Fidelity – Why I've Joined the WI

June 2014

As we approach the middle of 2014, I've been taking stock of my New Year's Resolutions, one of which was to join the WI (Women's Institute). I'd been mulling it over for years. I know a lot of ladies who belong, but few are in my immediate social group.

Until this year, the closest I'd got to joining was to buy an old WI brooch. I collect vintage enamel badges, and this one was a beauty – green, red and gold, bearing the organisation's original motto: "For Home and Country". This motto dates back to the year in which the WI was founded, 1915. In wartime conditions, and before women gained the right to vote, any British woman would surely have worn this badge with pride.

Nearly 100 years on, the WI has switched focus. Its current motto "Inspiring Women" is a great line, implying that its membership includes inspiring women, as well as working to inspire women.

Until I joined, I didn't realise just how active and pro-active the WI has become. It's too easy to dismiss its worth with the jokey shorthand of "Jam and Jerusalem", as my own experience demonstrates.

A few Christmases ago, I was all set to add "join WI" to my resolution list when through the letterbox came a little folded card, efficiently announcing the dates for the new year's meetings. Neatly printed on the back were the words for the hymn 'Jerusalem'. Much as I love the hymn, which we sung with gusto at every hymn practice in my primary school days, I allowed that resolution to fall off my list, unfulfilled.

But this year, I set aside my prejudice and joined. I knew that my author friend Sandy Osborne was coming from her home city of Bath to talk to our local group about her Bath-based novel *Girl Cop* (enjoyable for both men and women, I hasten to add). While visitors are allowed to attend any WI meeting without being obliged to join, I welcomed this prompt to make me sign on the dotted line.

I'm so glad I did. Joining the WI has been an eye-opener. I encountered a feisty, intelligent crowd with wide-ranging interests, energies and passions, and a refreshing curiosity. Not only is there a new topic for discussion each meeting, often with an engaging speaker from beyond the community, but there are also heaps of other activities throughout the month, from book groups to film clubs to walking parties. If I belonged to no other social group, I could easily fill my diary with stimulating activities purely from the WI. What a great way to make like-minded friends in your neighbourhood.

There are also opportunities to join other WIs for activities and to contribute to national campaigns. Last meeting included a lively discussion about organ donor policy.

I'm proud to be a member of the modern WI, which is definitely a force to be reckoned with – and if you don't believe me, just ask Tony Blair.

PS We've only sung 'Jerusalem' once, and nobody's yet mentioned jam.

School's Nearly Out for Summer

July 2014/August 2014

It's nearly time for school to be out for the summer, so why am I downhearted? Because the last day of term will mark the end of an era for me: my little girl will be leaving primary school for ever.

Really I should be celebrating. Laura has not only had the good fortune to attend an outstanding primary school, and I mean that in the OFSTED* sense, she's also gained a place at an excellent secondary school. I've enjoyed playing an active part in the life of her primary school, serving on the PTA for six years – I got time off for good behaviour this last year. But every parent I know who has children at senior school assures me that life will never be quite the same again.

With an aversion to change that is typical of her age, Laura is nervous of moving up, though less so with every step she takes towards it – completing SATS, visiting Open Days, planning her new school uniform. I'm sure that, by

September, she'll be eager to embrace the new opportunities that will come her way.

I know I was when I was her age. Gaining all the trappings of secondary school status was an exciting process, even if it was accompanied by my parents tutting at the expense. The smart new uniform and blazer, shiny leather satchel, a mysterious-looking geometry set in a tin, my own little hardback Oxford dictionary – all these heralded the start of a new adventure.

Although I don't remember my final day at primary school, I do recall sobbing as I got on the last school bus from my secondary school. I was living abroad, attending Frankfurt International School in Germany. The school was run on American lines, making much drama of our departure with a university-style graduation ceremony, complete with gowns and mortarboards.

I was voted "valedictorian", or class speaker, responsible for making a final address to the assembled parents and staff on behalf of the graduating students. I still have the typescript of my speech, which I'd bashed out on my red portable typewriter (no home computers in those days) and sellotaped onto orange sugar paper. I spoke about how attending an international school fit us better to play our part in the wider world.

The speech went down well. I remembered to speak slowly and clearly, as per the instructions I'd written to myself in big red letters around the edge; everyone laughed in the right places; and afterwards other people's parents asked for signed copies, assuring me that I'd be a famous writer before long. Well, we were all saying what each other wanted to hear that day.

Now, more years later than I care to confess, I've just published my very first fiction collection as an Amazon eBook called *Quick Change*. It contains twenty terse flash fiction pieces, arranged in chronological order by the age of each story's key characters, from cradle to grave. Pre-publication feedback is encouraging: "Very subtle, very English, very clever"; "Sly, witty, surprising, with genuine twists"; "[the stories] make domesticity look edgy, sometimes dangerous, but they are also life-affirming". So rather like the *Tetbury Advertiser*, don't you think?

I just hope Laura fulfils her ambitions a little faster than I did upon leaving school.

A Summer of Two Extremes

September 2014

I shall remember this summer break as the holiday of two extremes – scorching, dry sunshine and chill, torrential rain as I flitted from Ithaca to Inverness.

Our trip to Ithaca was a busman's holiday for me. I was helping run the Homeric Writers' Workshop and Retreat, so called because the island was the start and finishing point of perhaps the most famous journey of all: that of Odysseus, as chronicled by the ancient Greek master storyteller, Homer.

Our Scottish trip was occasioned by my husband's own odyssey – to climb all 282 Munros, the Scottish mountains of 3,000 feet or more, named after the man who first mapped them.

On Ithaca, the weather was idyllic: constant sunshine, cornflower-blue skies, refreshing sea breezes, all day, every day. The locals apologised that there were clouds in the sky – tiny Persil-white puffballs, apparently not usually seen between June and September.

A few days later, when we flew into Inverness to meet my husband (already there in our camper van, with 20 more Munros crossed off his list), steady rain was falling from steely skies. As we headed west for Ullapool, the clouds became more leaden. Linen sundresses, so comfortable on Ithaca, were supplemented with leggings, t-shirts, cardigans, shawls – all at once.

On Ithaca there are constant reminders to conserve water, always in short supply on this tiny island. In Scotland, there is evidence everywhere of the abundance of local water: high and raging rivers, waterfalls and landslips beside the roads. New flood defences are under construction wherever we go, and not a moment too soon. If there's ever a global shortage of water, Scotland's a dead cert for world domination.

Yet as we retreated southwards, I realised that my two holiday destinations weren't so different after all, and not just because they both prompted us to haemorrhage money on dubious souvenirs.

Both have a vast diaspora, thanks to economic migrants driven to North America, Australia, and South Africa by the Highland Clearances in Scotland and by the1953 earthquake in Ithaca.

Both landscapes are scarred by the ruins of abandoned simple stone houses, surprisingly similar in structure and appearance.

Both populations departed with a deep love of their homeland imprinted on their hearts. Whenever they can, they return. Australian, American and South African accents abound on Ithaca. In Scotland, 2014 has been declared Homecoming Year to mark the 700th anniversary of the Battle of Bannockburn, at which the Scots trounced the English. (By chance, my husband hails from Bannockburn.)

I feel privileged to have been able to holiday in places that so many people, all over the world, will always regard as home. Yet I'm also glad to return to the Cotswolds, which, as a small child on holiday there, I resolved I would one day make my home.

Because as Homer himself once said: "Nothing is sweeter than home". At least, that's what it says on my Ithacan souvenir fridge magnet.

[illegible]

A Month on the Wagon with Go Sober for October

October 2014

Earlier this year I reached that magical age when the NHS summons you for a personal MOT, to be repeated every five years, presumably until you're no longer roadworthy.

I'm always grateful to the NHS for the wonderful care that my family receives. But any self-respecting woman of – ahem – a certain age will understand my trepidation at the thought of a battery of questions and blood tests, an official weigh-in and a height check. The height test was not a problem: I was confident that I hadn't gained height. My weight, on the other hand, is precisely 20% more than it was when I was 20.

A week after the tests, I was called in to review the results with a nurse. My husband despatched me to the surgery with a knowing look, as if expecting me to be sent home with a diet sheet and a registration form for Alcoholics Anonymous. To his surprise, the nurse had only good news to report. I apparently have only a 3.5% risk in the next ten years of a cardiovascular event, a euphemism that makes a heart attack sound like an agreeable trip to the seaside.

"What about my nightly two glasses of wine?" I enquired. "Isn't that something I ought to change?"

"No, you're borderline, no problem," the nurse reassured me.

"And my BMI? I thought it was meant to be less than 25."

"No, we only really worry if it's over 30."

Well, that news certainly lowered my blood pressure. (It's a calm 100/60, if you're wondering.)

Her prescription for my future wellbeing: "Go home and treat yourself to a cream cake!"

Actually, I'm not keen on cream cakes, which is probably just as well, but I don't want my current state of health to make me complacent. Therefore shortly after my return from my appointment, I searched online for more information about a sponsored health-related campaign to which a friend of mine had alerted me earlier in the week. Raising funds for Macmillan Cancer Support, it's succinctly called "Go Sober for October". This isn't the first time it's been run, but in previous years I've clearly missed the boat – or rather, wagon.

Just as I was about to sign the pledge, into my email inbox dropped a message from the esteemed editor of this magazine:

"This month we'll be celebrating the fortieth anniversary of the *Tetbury Advertiser*!"

I'm hoping it won't go amiss if the glass I raise in its honour will be filled with nothing more than elderflower fizz? Here's to the good health of the *Tetbury Advertiser*!

Why I'm an Embarrassing Parent

November 2014

"Mummy, I never gave you my permission to put my picture on the cover of a book!"

So said my daughter Laura when I showed her the proof copy of my latest book, *Coming To Terms With Type 1 Diabetes*, to be launched in paperback this month to mark World Diabetes Day (14 November).

It's a lovely photo that captured her unawares, looking characteristically dreamy, described by her doting grandpa as "St Laura".

Now that Laura's at secondary school, I'm probably on borrowed time for posting her photos online or for writing about her exploits in public. I'd hate to become an embarrassing parent – to which her retort would probably be "Too late!"

In this case, however, the serious purpose behind the book justifies the use of her photo, with or without her permission: it's raising awareness of Type 1 Diabetes and funds for the search for a cure.

This serious incurable disease affects both Laura and my husband Gordon. Laura was diagnosed at the age of just three. Her diagnosis hit me like a bereavement, and I went through the classic stages of grief, from initial shock and denial to acceptance.

Determined not to let our family life be dictated by a medical condition, we have learned to move on in positive spirits and live life to the full. I hope that sharing our experience in this book will offer moral support to those in the same situation. It should also help others understand what it's like to live with Type 1 Diabetes without having to ask potentially embarrassing questions of those who have it.

Profits from sales of the book will be donated to JDRF, the leading charitable funder of Type 1 Diabetes research. The more funds raised, the closer we are to a cure – which is nowhere near as close as was misreported in the national press last month. Sigh.

If you'd like to come to the launch event, join me at Foyles Bookshop, Cabot Circus in Bristol, on 13 November from 6–7.30pm for an entertaining evening. Special guests include Paul Coker, who has just climbed Mount Kilimanjaro for JDRF to prove that having Type 1 doesn't stop you doing anything, and research scientist Dr Kathleen Gillespie, who will be telling us why good cooks make good lab researchers, and vice versa. That could add a whole new twist to the *Great British Bake Off*.

Christmas Surprises

December 2014/January 2015

Although we put so much effort into planning our festive celebrations, I often find the highlights of my Christmas are the moments that take me by surprise.

One such occasion occurred when I was a child, growing up in an outer suburb of London. When I was about 11, the age my daughter is now, I was for the first time considered old enough to go to the midnight church service on Christmas Eve. We weren't a particularly religious family, but the small, plain church in our garden suburb had special significance for us. My parents had married there, we children had been christened there, my grandfather was its choirmaster, and the small, rotund, gentle-mannered vicar, Mr Daniels, was a family friend.

The night was grey and drizzly as we entered the church, which seemed bright, warm and welcoming after our chilly walk from home. Though battling to stay awake, I enjoyed the service. I was especially impressed by the colourful model crib, but the most memorable moment was yet to come. When Mr Daniels threw open the heavy porch door for the congregation to leave, the churchyard before us lay covered in a perfect blanket of snow. Illuminated by the orange glow of street lamps, big flakes fell steadily as we gazed in wonder, never having guessed that the weather could change so much during the church service.

Yes, I know it didn't really snow in Bethlehem, but that snowfall felt like a special Christmas blessing: deep and crisp and even, snow on snow. You have to admire God's timing.

After serendipitous delights like this, I'm happy to leave much of my Christmas preparation to chance. An incurable last-minute merchant in any case, I know that nothing I could plan would ever surpass the wonder of the snowy walk home from church all those years ago.

My love of festive surprises influenced my latest book *Stocking Fillers*, a collection of twelve humorous short stories about the festive season. Each tale follows a different character as they prepare for Christmas, from a small boy who tries to give Santa time management lessons to an old lady celebrating what's likely to be her last Christmas. Though not all the characters are loveable, I hope you'll find them entertaining and memorable.

But you don't have to take my word for it. Just before writing this column, I received a lovely surprise – the first official review of the book, which describes it as follows:

"A delightful celebration of all things Christmas, *Stocking Fillers* features 12 funny, thoughtful, surprising and heart-warming tales that will get you in the festive spirit. Debbie Young's writing is thoroughly engaging. If you're looking to put some of the magic back into Christmas, and rediscover the reason for the season, start by treating yourself to this lovely read."

Well, that surprise has made my Christmas already.

I wish you a very Merry Christmas, and may it be filled with wonder and surprises of your own.

Putting the Up in Sidcup

February 2015

When I first visited the Cotswolds decades ago, I would have been one of 'those tourists'. Now that I've lived here for nearly a quarter of a century, a refugee from London suburbia, I realise the area is not as static as it looks. Edge-of-town superstores have effected a sea-change, while high streets evolve less perceptibly but just as unstoppably. I can't even remember now what preceded Tetbury's Tardis-like Yellow-Lighted Bookshop (was it the bike shop?), which feels and looks, in the nicest possible way, as if it's been there forever, and I'm glad that it is there. The same goes for Hobbs House Bakery.

While some changes will always be more welcome than others, it's natural to be sceptical and even fearful if too much changes too fast, even though change often brings fresh blood, new ideas and younger populations to keep cherished traditions and old institutions alive.

A recent trip to the land of my birth – Sidcup, Kent, on the edge of London's urban sprawl – made me look afresh at the nature of change in residential areas. Many years ago, I discovered that half the garden of the house I grew up in had been sold to developers. A three-bed semi on a corner plot in a 1930s garden suburb, it had the generous proportions that came as standard in an era when housebuilding land was cheap and plentiful. When subsequent owners built a new house on that plot, requiring the demolition of my old swing, my father's garage and his beautiful rose bed, I was outraged.

Revisiting just before Christmas with a more mature eye, I noticed that newcomers had added style, substance and care to the whole neighbourhood – double glazing, extensions, new doors, smart signage. Even the humble bungalow where I was born had been extended upwards and outwards and had expensive cars on the drive. As a child, I travelled everywhere by bus. The area had leapt upmarket, yet the many parks and green spaces remained. I found myself thinking, *What a lovely place to bring up a child!*

So I started the New Year feeling twice blessed for the double life I have led – half in the suburbs, half in the country – and grateful for the subtle changes that help both places to evolve and survive for future generations to enjoy.

Finally Facing My Waterloo

March 2015

Until last autumn, if in a word association game I had been given "Waterloo", I'd probably have responded "ABBA". I vividly remember watching the Swedish pop group win the Eurovision Song Contest in 1974 and thinking it was a life-changing moment. (In my defence, I was only 14.)

My second response would have been "Charing Cross", because Waterloo East was the next station out of London on the branch line to Sidcup, where I lived until the year of Abba's victory. And I'd defy anyone to think of the Duke of Wellington without also picturing Wellington boots.

I fear my historical ignorance adds point to the government's plan to focus the school history curriculum on major historic milestones. In my day, history lessons jumped from the Black Death to the First World War, leaving me to fill the void with details gleaned from books and museums. The most I knew about the Napoleonic Wars came from reading Tolstoy's *War and Peace* for a bet about 25 years ago.

This is why the Battle of Waterloo was low on my radar until just before Christmas, when a friend told me about the Waterloo Ball to be held at Westonbirt School on Friday 19 June to mark the Battle's bicentenary.

My crass response: "Who will know or care about that?" I recognise that in British eyes, the Battle of Waterloo is 'A Good Thing' because we won it, but for me it had much less resonance than last year's centenary of the outbreak of the First World War, with which I felt a personal connection. I had met relatives affected by it, such as my Great Great Auntie Edie, widowed at a young age by the Great War.

I've now realised the error of my ways. Especially in an election year, we should not underestimate the significance of what the Waterloo 200 campaign describes as "A Defining Moment in European History" in its strapline.

So in preparation for this great event, I'm reading up on it, with a local reference as my starting point: the Somerset Monument in Hawkesbury Upton, built to commemorate a local man's distinguished service at the Battle of Waterloo.

My research is already proving more entertaining than I'd expected, uncovering anecdotal gems such as the Duke of Wellington remarking to the Earl of Uxbridge, riding horseback beside him during the Battle, "By God, sir, you've lost your leg."

"By God, sir, so I have," came the reply.

Now that kind of British pluck is definitely worth celebrating.

Celebration Time

April 2015

Writing this month's column in the run-up to my parents' sixty-second wedding anniversary, I've been thinking about how we choose and mark the days we wish to celebrate.

My parents' choice of wedding date has always struck me as the romantic ideal: 21 March, the first day of spring, subtler and wiser than Valentine's Day. If a Valentine's marriage ends in divorce, that day is forever blighted with a reminder of rejection.

For some events we must take pot-luck. My brother had the good fortune to be born on Midsummer's Day – surely the perfect birthday, half way between two Christmases – whereas my sister's Trafalgar Day birthday was fitting for the first-born of my father, then serving in the Royal Navy.

When my grandmother asked my mother what she wanted for her tenth birthday, she said, "A baby brother", and my grandmother duly obliged, albeit on New Year's Eve – definitely a duff date for a birthday.

Some coincidences are less fortunate. My Scottish husband, born on St David's Day, landed a lifelong association with the wrong nation's patron saint.

On our school trip to Windsor Castle, my Greek friend Bill (short for Vasilios) realised he had the same birthday as Prince Charles when the resident band struck up "Happy Birthday to You". Now, when the National Anthem airs on BBC Radio 4 on the morning of HRH's birthday, I immediately think of Bill. Sorry, Sir!

For my first marriage, I thought I'd chosen a good date for my wedding: 4 August, the same day as my sister's. I'd not have done this had I known my new husband would die 10 years later, tinging my sister's future anniversaries with sadness.

Marrying for the second time, I picked a date with no prior associations: 2 April, inadvertently providing the opening joke for the best man's speech:

"When Gordon told me he was getting married on 2 April, I thought he was a day late". (He had been a confirmed bachelor until then.)

But who needs birthdays and anniversaries anyway? The best things in life are worth celebrating all year, any year. We may, for example, look forward to lionising the Lions (publisher of the *Tetbury Advertiser*) when they turn

100 years old (the organisation, not the individuals!) in 2017, but we don't have to save up our gratitude till then.

By the same token, on any day of the year, when I see my parents walking down the street, still holding hands after nearly 62 years of marriage, I throw metaphorical confetti. So today I wish them, and everybody like them, a very happy un-anniversary – and may there be many, many more.

Springing into Action

May 2015

The unseasonably warm weather after Easter makes me buck up my ideas about housework, a topic never front-of-mind for me. With spring sunshine streaming through smudgy windows, I can no longer pretend that it's fairy-dust adorning the piano.

I brace myself to brandish a duster and head for the under-sink cupboard. First task: awaken the cleaning materials from hibernation. Second task: dust the can of polish.

In search of a duster, I move aside a dozen blue, green and yellow bottles, mostly unopened since I bought them in an optimistic extension of the "new broom sweeps clean" theory. I've since decided that only applies to brooms, because brooms can be used straight after purchase without any more ado, unlike these fancy products, which require you to read small-print instructions and find accessories – cloths, sponges, buckets, or squeegees.

Some of the products I don't even recognise. Unable to remember buying them, I half-expect their price labels to be in shillings and pence. What a good thing they don't bear a use-by date.

In the absence of spring sunshine, the second best trigger for housework is to schedule a party, because my loathing of housework is exceeded by my fear of being branded a slob. Fear of a visitor's judgemental finger running through the dust on top of the piano spurs me into cleaning mode, but family fingers are less effective. The "Clean Me" message that my daughter wrote in the dust on my husband's laptop has lain undisturbed for several days.

This notion that the best way to get something done is to do something else is what I call "Janet's Principle", named after my sister-in-law, who once declared, just before serving us home-made apple pie, that "The best way to clean your nails is to make pastry".

In other areas of my life, I prefer a more direct route to results. One of my favourite mantras is "The best way to get something done is to do it". Or alternatively, hire a cleaning lady.

That option wouldn't have been open to the original working-class inhabitants of my Victorian cottage. Even so, they will have kept it much cleaner than I do, with little more than a broom, a rag, and some old-fashioned soapflakes. Our forefathers didn't need gimmicky modern products, because they had two vital ingredients that I so clearly lack: enthusiasm and elbow grease. I wonder what reaction I'd get if I asked for those in Tesco?

What's in a Car Name?

June 2015

Last month, the law of unintended consequences dictated that I should acquire a new car. Dropping in to a local garage to chivvy progress on my dad's car's MOT, I found myself wandering around its used car lot and falling in love at first sight with a Fiat Panda. If only actual pandas had the same impact on each other, there'd be a lot more pandas in this world.

For some time, I'd been meaning to replace my aging Ford Ka. It had a lot in common with the proverbial spade that the old man claims was his grandfather's before him – except the handle and the metal part have each been replaced several times.

Although I loved my Ford Ka, I'd been constantly irritated by its name. I could never decide whether to pronounce it to rhyme with "car" or as the initials K A. The only redeeming feature was the suffix "Sublime", in honour of its leather seats and air-conditioning.

In the same way that you get "Friday afternoon cars", haphazardly assembled by demob-happy workers, the Ford Ka brand name must be a Friday afternoon marketing job. It's about as sensible as Mr Kipling launching a new product called "Kayke", hard to differentiate from the rest of his exceedingly good cakes. (He hasn't done this yet, by the way – but, Mr Kipling, if you're reading this, please don't go there.)

But what's not to love about a car named after an iconic animal? Not to mention its endless potential for jokes.

"There's a panda in my front garden," I'm able to say to anyone gullible enough to listen to me speculating as to whether Waitrose stocks bamboo. Or "I'm thinking of taking my panda to the zoo at the weekend." You get the picture.

Other cars named after animals are usually associated with speed: Jaguar, Cougar, Impala. Even a beetle moves fast in relation to its size. Pandas are famously inert, as our visit to Edinburgh Zoo two summers ago hammered home: the crowd jumped the first time Tian Tian moved. Optimistically, the Zoo has installed a "panda cam" so you can watch live action footage around the clock. Most of the time, there's not much difference between the video and the still photo at the top of the webpage. If it's action you're after, click on "penguin cam" or "squirrel monkey cam". It must have been a close call in Fiat's marketing department one Friday between the Fiat Panda and the Fiat Sloth.

Still, it could have been worse: I could have opted for a Vauxhall Nova, which may sound fine and shiny-new till you drive to Spain, when it morphs into the Vauxhall Doesn't Go. Which is where I came in with my Ford Ka.

Booked Up for the Holidays

July/August 2015

As the *Tetbury Advertiser* prepares for its summer factory shutdown, I'm planning my holiday packing.

This task is straightforward, because most of our holidays are spent in our camper van, essentially a giant suitcase on wheels.

Or in my case, a mobile library. Because for me, packing clothes is a minor task compared with choosing my reading material. Books and writing essentials always form the bulk of my luggage. It's a good thing I don't have to worry about a baggage weight allowance.

Before each trip, I carefully assemble an assortment of books to complement my destination. First, essential reference books: a phrase book and dictionary for the language spoken at our destination. (Yes, even when we're going to Scotland – *Teach Yourself Gaelic* is permanently on board.) Next, maps and guide books. I learned this habit the hard way a few years ago, after arriving in France for a month-long trip with neither country map nor Rough

Guide. We certainly took the scenic route that holiday, though not always on purpose.

Then comes the leisure reading material: a combination of non-fiction and fiction. For this summer's trip to Scotland, I've stockpiled a biography (*The Lighthouse Stevensons*), a collection of nature essays by a Scottish journalist, some modern Scottish poetry, and a murder mystery set on a Scottish island. Most of these were purchased on previous trips to Scotland, local books being among my favourite souvenirs to collect en route.

My holiday reading planning strategy is so ingrained that I was startled to learn today from my nephew, Dan Gooding (a writer and librarian), that it's common advice to do the opposite: take books that contrast with wherever you're going. I should therefore now be packing tropical adventure stories, gourmet food guides and biographies celebrating Tory MPs.

Other friends prefer to pick a particular writer and work their way through his or her complete oeuvre. My author friend Calum Kerr chooses a thriller writer every summer. My old English teacher spent one summer reading Proust's *A La Recherche Du Temps Perdu*. Well, you'd need a teacher's holidays to get through that lot.

One busy friend subcontracts the decision. Having time to read only when she's on holiday, she allows her mother and sister, both year-round readers, to lend her any books they think she'd like. It's like having a personal shopper for clothes, except she doesn't have to buy anything.

A kind teacher I know takes second hand paperbacks bought from charity shops and leaves them behind for others to enjoy. My brother-in-law uses this approach with holiday clothes, taking his oldest and tattiest so he needn't bother bringing them home. Of the two, I know whose wake I'd rather follow.

So why not splash out on some paperbacks from one of Tetbury's charity shops? That way you not only gain great new reads, but also help a good cause. When you leave them behind after reading at your holiday destination, you'll not only lighten your luggage for your journey home, but also leave plenty of space for holiday souvenirs.

The Library, the Witch and the Wardrobe

September 2015

On arrival at their holiday cottage on Brownsea Island, Dorset, the birthplace of Scouting and Guiding, what do you think was the biggest hit with my daughter's Girl-Guiding unit? Spotting copious red squirrels, finding exotic tail feathers dropped by the resident peacocks, or discovering the beach at the end of the garden?

Trick question! Actually, it was finding an ancient wooden wardrobe in each dormitory.

"I'm just off to Narnia!" the girls would call, taking it in turns to step inside the wardrobe. Their imagination did the rest to keep them entertained.

Variations on the game soon arose.

"Our wardrobe takes us to Rainbow Land."

"Ours leads to Hogwarts."

Did C S Lewis realise what a timeless icon he had created with that wardrobe? Surely the promise of a secret world of adventure behind a mundane facade is never far from the thoughts of anyone who has ever read *The Lion, The Witch and The Wardrobe* – or is that just me?

Only the other day it struck me while taking the shortcut to Tetbury Library that the winding, blinkered alleyway leading away from the hubbub of the shopping streets provides a Narnia-like transportation to a secret oasis of calm. As when entering the fabled wardrobe, those crossing the library's threshold will find different adventures according to their character and attitude. But unlike Narnia, where it is always winter but never Christmas, in a public library it is always Christmas. Any day you visit, you can walk away laden with gifts: books to read on free loan, DVDs, games and invitations to courses and events. All you need is the courage to open the wardrobe door and step inside, and, with faith, you'll find what you're looking for. And if you're not sure what you're seeking, you'll be readily assisted by expert librarians, who are not likely to resemble Mr Tumnus or Mr and Mrs Beaver in appearance, but they will share their generous and resourceful nature and specialist knowledge.

Only if there are enough people keeping the faith will libraries like Tetbury's survive. Otherwise they will slowly morph into just another lost mythological world. I hesitate to imagine the conversation with my grandchildren years from now.

"Yes, that's right, dear. The books were all free. Thousands of them, there were, on every subject and in every genre."

"Yet people just didn't bother using them?"

"Yes, dear, and that's why they shut them down."

To me, closing a public library is as unthinkable as locking the Professor's wardrobe and throwing away the key. Who would want to live in a society in which the most adventure to be had from a wardrobe is assembling an IKEA flat-pack?

By the way. I'm reliably informed that there are no witches in Tetbury Library. I'm not so sure about IKEA.

Queen, Cousin, Bishop – My Topical Take on Rock, Paper, Scissors

October 2015

Was I the only person holding their breath last month till the moment the Queen officially became our country's longest serving monarch? Knowing my Scottish husband's Republican tendencies, I kept to myself my anxiety that the Queen would fall at the last fence (a metaphor of which she would surely approve), until my daughter (12) piped up out of the blue "So exactly what time did the old King die? I don't want to celebrate too soon."

No matter what your political beliefs, you'd have to be hard hearted not to feel pleased on Her Majesty's behalf. I always love feeling that I'm living through a historical landmark moment that will be chronicled by historians and taught in the classroom to future generations of schoolchildren. No monarch is an island, and her achievement surely touches us all, in the same way that we can't help but feel a little fillip of excitement (no, not that sort of Philip) and ownership when our country wins a major sporting award, even if we usually take no interest in the game.

But the Queen's longevity was dwarfed a few days later by our visit to my late grandmother's cousin Nina (99). (Cousin trumps queen.) On our journey to her elegant seaside apartment (I think HRH would feel right at home there), it occurred to me that at the time of the Queen's coronation, Nina would already have considered herself middle-aged, having been born during the First World War. Greeting Nina feels like hugging history. (Thank goodness that modern standards have shunted our definition of midlife to a much older age. I'm in my prime, I'll have you know!)

A few days later, a local historic landmark put even Nina's longevity into perspective: the consecration of Rachel Treweek as the first female Bishop of Gloucester. (Bishop takes cousin.) I caught an interview on BBC *Woman's Hour* with her ecclesiastical garment designer, Polly Meynell, who observed that at her enthronement, Bishop Rachel will become the first woman to wear the bishop's cope (cloak), worn exclusively by men for the last 1,000 years. I just hope she gets to launder it first.

Votes for Minions

November 2015

Today I did two things I'd never done before: I went to the cinema alone, and I saw a film on the day of its general release.

Though I'd wanted to see *Suffragette* for ages, I don't usually get round to seeing films until they're out on DVD, unless they're children's movies such as *Minions*, the bright yellow and blue merchandise of which is everywhere just now.

This time I had an incentive to be quicker off the mark: my historian friend Lucienne Boyce, author of *The Bristol Suffragettes*, was to give a talk at the cinema before the film. In a show of support, and because I'm genuinely interested in the movement's history, I donned an outfit in suffragette colours (green, purple and white) – though I drew the line at chaining myself to the cinema railings.

I invited my daughter (12) to join me, but she decided the film wasn't relevant to her, because "We've had the vote for ages now, Mummy". I was glad that she felt so secure in her equal rights, yet for me the British Suffragette Movement feels like recent history. My grandmother didn't get the vote till she was 28. She was born in 1900, and in the UK, women only gained equal voting rights with men in 1928. While I was still at primary school, Grandma made me promise to use my vote and use it wisely. When I pressed her to tell me which party she voted for, she refused to say, citing the confidentiality of the ballot box.

The credits at the end of *Suffragette* include a list of the dates when women were granted the vote around the world. Though Britain lagged behind some countries, other nations made their women wait much longer, e.g. in Switzerland until 1971. Yes, 1971. Less surprisingly, Saudi Arabia's women are still only on a promise, and even that's just for local elections.

Even if, like my daughter, you think women's suffrage is old news, the film relays many topical messages about standing up for what you believe in, about giving voice to the oppressed, and about how far you should go to fight for your rights.

Though unhappy about the way the film ended (I won't spoil the plot in case you haven't seen it yet), I left the cinema buzzing with enthusiasm and laden with promotional flyers, badges and stickers bearing authentic suffragette slogans such as “Find Your Voice” and “Deeds Not Words”. I was even given a sash proclaiming “Votes for Women”. Oh, I do love souvenirs!

When I took my booty home, I expected my daughter to nab the stickers to adorn her school history book, but she declined. Fortunately, I had another conscience present for her up my sleeve: a small golden heart-shaped badge, sold at the box office in aid of the Variety Club children’s charity. This she was very happy to accept. The reason? It featured a Minion. Of course.

What's in a Book Title?

December 2015/January 2016

Now that we've made it past Halloween and Guy Fawkes Night, I'm spending a little time each day promoting my festive book, *Stocking Fillers*.

I intended the title to signal that it contains short stories to avoid upsetting any readers who feel short-changed by fiction that isn't in the form of a novel. Only after the book was published did I appreciate the subliminal helpfulness of a title that is also a serving suggestion: "Makes a great, er, stocking filler", as I have been known to tweet.

At any time of year, the choice of a book title is a sensitive issue for an author and a make-or-break decision for publishers, who will spike an author's preference if it's not commercial. Not that a title is an infallible predictor of sales: *Best Seller*, by Timothy B Sagges, languishes in obscurity.

The Last Man In Europe smacks to me of smug tabloid phraseology, reminiscent of *The Sun*'s infamous 1992 headline, "If Kinnock wins today, will the last person to leave Britain please turn out the lights". In 1948, George Orwell's publishers preferred *1984*, which quickly passed into popular culture as shorthand for an oppressive, controlling regime. Yet if a book with that title were published today, we'd assume it was a nostalgic memoir of the year in which Sweden won the Eurovision song contest with a song called *Diggi-Loo, Diggi-Ley*. Now there's a title of questionable judgement, unlike their compatriots' all-conquering *Waterloo* ten years before.

Which leads us neatly into consideration of *All's Well that Ends Well*, an inappropriately cheery working title for the huge, serious philosophical tome about the Napoleonic Wars eventually published as Tolstoy's *War and Peace.*

Even the most carefully chosen titles for international classics can cause confusion. Or is it just me? Until I read it for the first time this autumn, I didn't latch on to the significance of Harper Lee's title, *To Kill A Mockingbird* (originally written as *Atticus*). Then part way through the book, Miss Maudie explains it's a sin to kill a mockingbird because it does nothing but give people pleasure. It's thus a symbol of innocence destroyed. Dare I confess that I'd previously assumed a mockingbird to be an annoying parrot-like mimic, an unsurprising target for any short-fused American with easy access to handguns?

It's not easy to come up with names that work around the world and across cultures. Vauxhall found out the hard way that in Spanish, *Nova* means "doesn't go". I discovered too late that in the US, people prefer the term "stocking stuffers" to the one I've used for my festive book title. If it wasn't for its Christmassy cover, they might presume my book is all about legs.

I'd like to thank the team behind the perfectly-named *Tetbury Advertiser* for another year of dedication, hard work, patience and good humour, and to wish you all a very merry Christmas and a happy and healthy 2016. See you next year!

Acknowledgements

First and foremost, I must say a huge thank you to the present editor of the *Tetbury Advertiser* Richard Smith and his predecessor Barry Gibbs for their encouragement and support for my writing, and for publishing my columns for the last six years.

For the beautiful cover illustration of this book, I have to thank my very talented father, who took up painting, among many other hobbies, in retirement. His achievements give hope to us all for our old age.

I must thank my editor, Alison Jack, for polishing my prose with her usual efficiency and good nature.

Finally, I'd like to thank all those readers of the *Tetbury Advertiser* who have told me how much they've enjoyed my columns, encouraging me to keep sharing my thoughts this way. Your kind comments always make my day.

Debbie Young

Thank you for reading
YOUNG BY NAME

If you enjoyed this book, please consider leaving a brief review on Amazon, Goodreads or any website you prefer. Or stick to old technology and just tell your friends about it! Any recommendations will help more people find this book and enjoy it as you did.

You might also like to try the companion volume to this book, ***All Part of the Charm***, a collection of essays and columns about life in the nearby village of Hawkesbury Upton, written in a similar vein to those in this volume.

Alternatively you may enjoy my collections of short stories, available in paperback and ebook:

Marry in Haste

Quick Change

Stocking Fillers

For more information about my books and to follow my blog, please visit my website:

www.authordebbieyoung.com